This book is lovingly dedicated to the memory of my mother, Betty Lee, whose grace, wisdom, and timeless elegance still guides me with every step I take.

TABLE
of
CONTENTS

Part Three | pg. 91
Dining Etiquette

Part Four | pg. 137
Professional Etiquette and Business Success

Part Five | pg. 205
Digital World Etiquette

INTRODUCTION

This book is the culmination of both my life's journey and my work. I was so terribly shy and introverted when I was younger. My mom did everything she could to help me. I started out in charm school, then Blue Birds, then Girl Scouts, and by the time I was a senior in high school, I participated in my first pageant. I was really off to the races from there. I got the pageant bug, and every pageant I participated in had an etiquette component to it.

I spent my early years taking classes for my own personal development. I was a flight attendant for Continental Airlines for ten years, and I went through the International Etiquette and Protocol Training. Eventually, I started teaching others and creating this lifelong body of work. I have spent countless hours researching and studying for more than twenty years. I have done surveys. I have done studies. I have interviewed people from different industries and also everyday folks. I get questions sent to me through my website, through social media, and through all of my media appearances as well. This book is a culmination of all of that.

But here's my truth. There was a moment in this process when I could not move forward. I felt paralyzed, not by lack of passion, but by being overwhelmed. Emails from my editor, my cover designer, even my illustrator went unanswered. After some time and real reflection (and some counseling), I came to understand that my brain was doing what it needed to do. It was protecting me. I was overwhelmed, and so it shut down. I wasn't overwhelmed by the work itself. I think I was overwhelmed by the gravity of the work. I knew that I was creating something to shift the narrative of old-world etiquette and really set in stone a guide for this century.

That pause was well needed. It reminded me of what grace really looks like. It is not perfection, but persistence. When I came back to this work, I came back with clarity, with care, and with a renewed commitment to finish what I started.

Once I got back to writing the book, I kept imagining you. A person who is coming into the age of life where you are starting to carve out your own path and make a concerted effort to determine who you are as an individual. You know, we grow up with so many different parts of our family ingrained in us, customs, rituals, and other traditions. But at some point in time, we eventually begin to venture out on our own. We take our past experiences, and we want to shape ourselves. I kept seeing someone who wants to shape themselves, who wants to do better, be better, live better, be well, and live well. You are someone who sees the world through your own lens, and you want to show up in the world and make your mark. You want to be respected, and you want to do things with grace and style.

I think this particular book is needed right now because our world is changing quickly or it has changed. We need to look at what the new standard is. Etiquette has evolved over the century, and because etiquette has evolved, I believe we need to have a standard that represents what our world looks like today. Many years ago, we did things one way, but it has shifted. We have folks who are born into technology. The guidelines and nuances around that have to be solidified, the information needs to be shared, and we all need to get on one accord. Now is the time for us to have a resource that we can all turn to and utilize as a gold standard.

When you have finished reading this book, I want you to feel fully equipped to take on any social circumstance. I want you to feel empowered to stand in confidence. There is a difference between being comfortable and appearing confident.

Sometimes, just knowing what to do in a particular instance will allow you to appear confident. That will cause people to respond to you in a positive way. If you have what you need, if you know what you're supposed to do, you can focus less on asking yourself if you are messing up or not doing things correctly and focus more on having a positive impact on others.

What makes this book relevant and uniquely mine is that I have grounded it in what we are actually experiencing today. I am looking less at rules and more about impact. Impact on how we make others feel. Impact on how we show up in the world. Impact on the legacy that we are leaving behind. There are some things that are quite traditional. I mean, how to sit in a chair is still how to sit in a chair. But how we communicate with one another has definitely shifted and changed over the years. We have to know how to navigate those things differently. This book is not filled with me telling you about what used to be or how things used to go. You likely were never even taught things about white gloves and men tipping their hats and all that old stuff, so there is no need for me to unteach it. Instead, I want to provide you with relevant information that is forward, useful, and empowering for today's modern world.

It was my desire to write a book that would make you feel included. It is not so far-fetched that it feels like it is only for high society or folks who are privileged. This book is written for everyone. I believe in the approach, not only in the information I share, but the way I share is meant to help you feel included. That is an important part of what is meaningful to people today.

During the process of writing this book, I learned not only about myself, but I learned about you. I spent a lot of time researching to gain understanding about what your struggles are and what types of questions you have. I crafted this book so that you have actual answers, not fluff, but information that applies to your everyday life and even to those occasional moments you will encounter. I really looked at what you come in contact with on a regular basis and built from there.

I started this book with some key foundational aspects of etiquette and social behavior that will help elevate your personal and your professional presence. Some things I really enjoyed writing were the business and travel sections. I do not know if that has to do with the fact that I travel so often or that I was a flight attendant, but all of the nuances that go along with travel today have changed so much over the years. I really took joy in trying to illuminate how to do it with ease.

I also really enjoyed the dining etiquette portion. I felt relieved to let you know that it is perfectly fine to take pictures at the table. Twenty years ago, we were telling people to leave their cell phones in the car. It felt really great to illuminate that permission in that aspect.

Naturally, I am an event planner in terms of hosting. I love to host people in my home, and it is such an intricate part of who I am as an individual. I really enjoyed breaking down all the aspects of hosting a celebration in your home. Following these guidelines will help you get it right every time.

And then the wedding portion. I was a wedding coordinator for ten years, and that was what I did the first ten years of my etiquette business. I worked with brides a lot. A wedding is one of the biggest events of our lives.

I really liked tackling some of the questions that people are actually dealing with today. There is so much steeped in tradition when it comes to weddings, but a lot of what I shared reflects modern challenges based on what our world looks like today. Things like whether you invite your ex to the wedding, or can you bring a plus-one even if one was not included.

You may notice that some etiquette principles appear in more than one section of this book. That is intentional. Not every reader will explore each part, so I have included key tips where they are most relevant, whether you are navigating a dinner party or a business mixer. Think of it as a gentle reminder, tailored to the moment.

As you continue to go deeper into this book, I believe you're going to come out on the other side with answers, tools, resources, and real-life examples you can apply immediately to your life in so many different ways. I want you to walk away feeling like you have a resource you can turn to, review, study, apply, and practice—one that leaves you feeling charged, refreshed, and empowered. I want you to get really excited and say, *"Okay, this is it. This is the answer I was looking for."*

Now, let's step into the world of modern etiquette—together.

PART ONE

Everyday Life and Personal Presence

MASTERING DAILY INTERACTIONS
WITH GRACE AND CONFIDENCE

It is important to understand how your behavior may impact other people.

- ELAINE SWANN -

CHAPTER 1

Everyday Interactions and Introductions

In everything we do, it is important to understand how your behavior may impact other people. The foundation of etiquette begins within us as individuals. The moment we arise and begin to interact with the world each day, our presence and our behavior speak for us before we even say a word. It doesn't matter whether you are at home, at work, at the grocery store, or even at a neighborhood event, the way we interact with others says quite a bit about who we are as individuals. This section is about cultivating self-awareness and refining the way we show up. It explores how intentional behaviors can make a big difference in whether we impact people from a positive or negative perspective. You'll explore introductions, body language, grooming, and the art of making others feel comfortable in your presence. Because ultimately, good manners aren't something that we put on and take off each day, it's something that should be part of our innate makeup. It's a muscle we need to use regularly, so when it's time to show up, we arrive as the best version of ourselves.

INTRODUCTIONS

Whether you are being introduced or introducing another individual, it is very important to know the protocol surrounding it. You can set the tone for any interaction based upon the way you begin an introduction.

The proper way to introduce yourself to a room of people you do not know is to follow these instructions:

1.   If you are sitting, it is proper to stand up.

   • You command a more positive presence.

2.   Say your first and last name.

   • This is your first opportunity to establish who you are. Be complete in doing so.

3.   Tell the people something about yourself.

   • You can share something nice or simply follow any instructions given to you by the leader if you are at a group event.

WHEN INTRODUCING YOURSELF TO SOMEONE

Stand (if you are not already), smile, give a pleasant greeting, a firm handshake, and say, "Hello, my name is (state your first and last name)."

Leave out your title; you don't want to appear pretentious. That information can be revealed at another time.

WHEN YOU ARE THE INTRODUCER

1. Give a bit of information about the individual.

2. State their full name.

3. Use their title if they have one: Military Rank, Dr., Professor, Governor, etc.

4. Talk to the more important person first: "Dr. Medical, please meet my friend, Nice Neighbor."

5. And because clients are always most important: "Client, please meet my boss Vernetta Shine."

6. Group Introductions: "Everybody, this is Betty Lee." or "Betty, I'd like you to meet my friends from fitness class." Then allow everyone to introduce themselves individually later.

CONCERNING NAMES

In formal settings, it's best to use a person's last name until you're invited to use their first.

If you forget someone's name? Just ask! You might even add, "In case you don't remember, my name is (state your name)." This will help take the edge off their possible embarrassment or disappointment if they don't remember your name.

If a person has a difficult name to pronounce, just ask them to repeat their name. If you expect to meet them again, you might ask for a business card. Try to repeat their name during the conversation.

It's alright to correct the person if they mispronounce your name; just repeat it politely.

MEETING NEIGHBORS

If you see your new neighbors for the very first time, rather than say hello from afar, walk over and introduce yourself.

If people come to your home to welcome you to the neighborhood, rather than standing in the doorway, invite them in. Don't be offended if they decline; they may just want to keep their visit brief.

Both you and your partner or spouse should remain present during the visit, even if you only have one visitor. They came over to meet you both.

Stay engaged with the conversation; don't allow yourself to drift off into other household activities. Stay put during the entire visit.

Be mindful of what you say. Don't go into any complaining or gossip about other neighbors or the neighborhood itself. You never know who knows who.

Whether or not they bring a gift, be sure to follow up with a thank-you card expressing your appreciation for their time.

If you have a planned visit from a neighbor, follow a few simple guidelines to make your guests feel welcome. When they arrive at your home for the first time, be sure you create a pleasant environment. Tidy up a bit, light a candle, and be sure you don't have the television or other entertainment devices blaring.

If you have pets, put them outside or in another room.

It's a nice gesture to offer a simple beverage. There is no need to go overboard with snacks or food. Water, iced tea, or fruit juice are perfectly fine.

Pay attention to the body language of the individual. Be mindful of when it's time to wrap up the visit. You don't want to keep them hostage as you drone on and on with conversation.

FACE MASKS AND EVERYDAY COURTESY

Wearing a face mask in public is no longer unusual in the United States. While this practice was once primarily associated with countries like Japan, where wearing a mask is considered a common courtesy during cold and flu season, it has become a normal and personal choice for many Americans following the COVID-19 pandemic.

If you see someone wearing a mask, do not ridicule or question them. Simply respect their decision. They may be protecting themselves or protecting you.

Likewise, if you choose to wear a face mask, be polite and avoid pressuring others to adopt the same practice. Everyone's comfort level is different, and mutual respect goes both ways.

HOW TO ADDRESS PEOPLE

There are many ways to address authority figures and officials. When you speak respectfully, it shows maturity and encourages others to treat you the same way.

Growing up, you may have been taught not to call adults by their first name, like saying "Ms. Elaine." That's still fine as an adult. It shows a polite, endearing form of respect.

1. Addressing adults verbally

   - Adult male: Mr. *(pronounced Mister)*
   - Adult female, married: Mrs. *(pronounced Miss-iz)*
   - Adult female, unmarried or in the business arena: Ms. *(pronounced Miz)*
   - When uncertain of marital status, use Ms.

2. When any official has a military rank or a doctoral degree, use the proper title instead of Mr., Mrs., or Ms.

3. In written communication with adults, always spell out all titles in the address except Dr., Mr., and Mrs.

4. When writing to adults who have a title, such as Doctor, do not use two titles with the same meaning. For example:

   - WRONG – Doctor Jane Doe, M.D.
   - CORRECT – Jane Doe, M.D. or Dr. Jane Doe

5. In written communication with children, use the following forms:

   - Female: Always use Miss
   - Male Ages 1–12: Master (Example: Master John Doe)
   - Male Ages 12–18: Their first and last name (Example: John Doe)

1. When to use the title The Honorable

   - All Presidential appointees and Federal- and State-elected officials.

   - All Mayors.

   - As a general rule, county and city officials are not addressed as The Honorable.

   - A person once entitled as Governor, Senator, Judge, General, The Honorable, or similar title may retain the title throughout his or her lifetime.

2. The title Madam is used before formal terms such as:

   - President

   - Vice President

   - Chairman

   - Secretary

   - Ambassador

   - Minister

3. Senators and members of U.S. House of Representatives

   - Senator – A female member of the U.S. Senate

   - Senator-elect – A woman who has been elected to the Senate but not yet sworn in

   - Congresswoman – A female member of the U.S. House of Representatives

   - Congresswoman-elect – A woman who has been elected but not yet sworn in

SHAKING HANDS

If you are ever meeting or greeting someone and you have to shake hands, never shake hands from a seated position. Always stand up. When you stand, you position yourself in a more elevated presence, and you set a standard for respect and authority.

- Stand up straight, hold your head high, and look directly at the person.

- Always shake with your right hand.

- A proper handshake is always web to web.

- Shake the person's hand once or twice, then let go.

- Be mindful not to squeeze the other person's hand. This could give the impression that you are aggressive and inconsiderate.

- Do not shake hands with a limp or just your fingers. This may send a message that you are too passive and uninterested.

- This is the proper greeting in the United States, regardless of age or gender.

Traditional Handshake

ALTERNATIVES TO THE TRADITIONAL HANDSHAKE

If you'd prefer not to shake hands, there are courteous alternatives you can use without seeming rude or standoffish. A quick fist bump is a casual, respectful option that's now widely accepted. You can also place your palms together in the prayer hands gesture or simply keep your hands clasped in front of you. Accompany the gesture with a warm smile and a polite explanation, such as, "I'm not shaking hands right now, but it's a pleasure to meet you" is perfectly acceptable in both personal and professional settings.

Fist Bump

Praying Hands

CHAPTER 2

Social Confidence and Communication

EYE CONTACT

When speaking to someone, it is important to look at them rather than at the ground, a practice known as good eye contact. However, maintaining eye contact does not mean staring directly into a person's eyes. To stay visually connected for a longer period, you can focus on their forehead, eyebrows, nose, or chin.

CONVERSATION SKILLS

Using complete sentences when answering questions is essential for clear and polite communication. For example, if someone asks, "Where do you live?" rather than responding with a single word like "Oceanside," it is better to say, "I live in Oceanside." Similarly, if asked, "How many kids do you have?" instead of replying with "Four," say, "I have four children."

Proper greetings are also an important aspect of etiquette.

When greeting someone you have met before, be sure to acknowledge them politely by saying, "Hello" or "It's nice to see you again." If you are meeting someone for the first time, an appropriate greeting would be, "How do you do?" or "It's nice to meet you."

SMALL TALK

Refine your self-introduction. Use every opportunity to practice. It should feel natural, not like a sales pitch. Just keep it brief, friendly, and sincere.

Stay informed. Read up on current events, industry news, and pop culture. You never know when a celebrity headline or trending topic might come up in conversation. Being well-rounded helps you connect more easily and keeps things from feeling awkward.

Be positive. Never criticize the host, the venue, or the food. You could be talking to the caterer.

Keep your body language open. I've seen a lot of people who look like ice kings and queens at social events. They stand with stern facial expressions. Others cross their arms, wring their hands, stand against the wall, or bite their nails. Instead, walk in with a smile. Keep your hands to your sides. And remember, if you don't look or act nervous, people won't know you are nervous.

Have the courage to converse. Plan conversation starters and know how to find areas of interest by listening to the conversation. Remember, everyone loves to talk about themselves.

Use key starters to get the conversation going. You can say:

- How did you hear about the event?

- How do you know (the person of honor)?

- How long have you lived in the area?

Ask questions to encourage the other person to talk. Comment on their answers to continue the conversation. Here are four types of comments you can make:

- Expanding: "Tell me more! It sounds as if you had a great time."

- Comparing: "That sounds as if it is similar to . . ."

- Self-revealing: "I know what you mean. I was in a similar situation last year."

- Clarifying: "What exactly did he/she do?"

Avoid talk that is critical or confidential. It's sometimes easy to relax a bit more when you're in a casual environment, but remember to keep a well-poised demeanor. The slightest slip of the tongue can be carried away by another individual and cause you problems later.

Avoid discussing political, religious, or lifestyle issues. You'll just end up irritating people, and this is the easiest way to get into an argument, especially when fueled by alcohol. Unless the group is of the same affiliation, keep your opinions about those issues to yourself.

Ask people their opinions. Don't spend the whole time talking about what's important to you; slow down and ask the person their opinion about what's being said. Be sure to avoid asking yes or no questions. This way, you'll stimulate and encourage more conversation.

Listen, listen, listen. You'll learn more about a person when you actually listen to what's being said rather than just being silent as you wait for your turn to talk. Focus on the person who is talking and try to tune out the other distractions around you.

Practice, practice, practice. Practice talking to people whom you would consider to be "safe" (meaning non-business). Practice chatting with your neighbor and people in line at the bank or grocery store. The more you practice, the more comfortable you'll become talking with people you don't know.

Use exit lines. Not only do you need to say hello, but you also need to say goodbye. An exit line will help you say goodbye gracefully and leave on a positive note. Don't strive for cleverness. Just be sincere. You can simply say, "Nice talking to you. I'm going to say hello to a few more folks," "Good to see you! I'm going to mingle for a little while," or "I hope to see you again soon."

SOCIAL AWARENESS

Social awareness is the ability to understand and respect the perspectives of others and apply them to your interactions. Additionally, it is important to understand how your behavior may impact other people. Social awareness also includes being in tune with other individuals' body language. This is a form of communication that is nonverbal. It's important that we pay attention to the way people behave (nonverbal cues) in order to determine how they might feel.

Sounds: Sighing, laughing, humming, gasping.

Closeness: Standing too close, stepping back, maintaining a comfortable distance.

Body contact: Patting on the back, shaking hands, hugging, bumping into someone.

Facial expressions: Raised eyebrows, a frown or a smile, a neutral face, pursed lips.

Posture: Standing tall, leaning forward, slouching, drooped shoulders, crossing arms.

Appearance: Well-groomed, wearing bright colors, untidiness, wrinkled clothes.

Ways of talking: Speaking quickly, mumbling, pauses or stress on words, speaking clearly.

Hand movements: Clapping, pointing, rubbing hands together, waving.

Eye movements: Rolling eyes, staring, avoiding eye contact, winking or blinking.

Head movements: Shaking head, tilting head, looking down, nodding.

HOW TO BE PRESENT, APPROACHABLE, AND ENGAGED AT EVENTS

- The way we carry ourselves sends a message to others.

- Choose attire that fits well, looks great, and is appropriate for the setting.

- Be mindful of how your clothing choices might be perceived.

- Win people over with your hospitality. Be open, helpful, and approachable.

- Step in and assist when you see a need, as it makes you more welcoming to others.

- Give yourself permission to leave social events early if you need to.

- If you are in an environment where you don't know many people, connect with someone in advance to make the experience more enjoyable.

- Don't spend the entire event on your phone.

- Drink in moderation so that your presence reflects poise, not overindulgence.

CHAPTER 3

Grace, Posture, and Personal Conduct

WALKING, STAIRS, AND ESCORTING

The way you walk has much to do with how you present yourself. Walk with genuine pride and confidence. You will make a positive impression, and people will respond to you in a more respectful manner.

Keep your chin level to the floor. Keep your arms natural. Try to walk while maintaining a good posture. Pay attention to your feet.

When walking on a people mover in the airport, always walk to the left and stand to the right. When walking on a sidewalk, be mindful of others who are around you trying to pass by.

When a male and female approach a revolving door, the male goes first to push the door through. Traditionally, when a male is walking with a female, it's polite for him to walk on the curb side of the street.

When going up a staircase, the female goes up first and the male follows behind. When going down a staircase, the male goes down first and the female follows behind. If the stairs are wide enough, it is acceptable for them to ascend and descend side by side.

If a male is escorting a female, for example at a formal dance or a wedding, he holds his left arm at his waist and offers it to the female. She places her right hand on top of his left hand or at the crook of his arm.

Arm-in-Arm Escort   *Hand-in-Hand Escort*

STANDING

Always stand when you are being introduced. When approached and addressed by an older person, women and men should always stand.

Whether greeting someone, entering a room, or observing a moment of silence, your posture shows respect and attentiveness.

When you are in a foreign country, it is always polite to stand during that country's national anthem.

When in the presence of senior citizens, younger people do not sit until the elder person is seated.

When sitting at the table with a female, the male should always stand when she stands and then sit once she has left. When she returns to the table, he should stand again and then sit after she has resumed her seat.

When in the presence of a female who is standing, a male should not sit down. In this instance, ladies should be mindful of the amount of time they are standing to not inconvenience others.

HOW TO SIT IN A CHAIR

Whether you are visiting someone's house, at a restaurant, or attending a special event, it's always important to sit in a respectful manner.

As you approach a chair to sit in it, turn with your back facing the chair. Lower yourself into the chair (no "plopping"). Ladies, smooth out your dress or skirt (if you're wearing one).

As you are sitting, keep your feet flat on the floor and maintain a straight but relaxed posture. Aim to keep your knees together as best you can, or cross your legs at the ankle. Avoid crossing at the knee, as it can reveal too much in a short skirt and may sometimes send the wrong message through body language.

When you are sitting in front of an audience, it is not necessary to sit all the way back against the chair. You may move slightly forward to avoid the appearance of slouching.

HOW TO PICK SOMETHING UP FROM THE FLOOR

For ladies, the proper way to pick something up off the floor is to bend down at the knees and not at the waist. The reason it is best to do this is because if you are wearing a short skirt, it might rise and show your undergarments. If you are wearing pants, the portion around your waist might slide down, showing too much skin. You can kneel with both knees or just one, whichever is best for your agility. Bending at the knees helps you to keep your appearance in check and present yourself in a modest manner.

With social kisses, your lips should not touch anyone's face. Appropriate kisses are cheek to cheek or air to air.

EVERYDAY COURTESIES AND PUBLIC BEHAVIOR

When greeting others, whether in person, over the phone, or in writing, it's important to consider the time of day. Choosing the appropriate greeting demonstrates awareness, warmth, and consideration, all of which are essential to modern etiquette.

Use these guidelines to help you choose the right time-of-day greeting.

Guidelines for Time-of-Day Greetings:

- "Good Morning" → Until 12:00 p.m. (noon)

- "Good Afternoon: → From 12:00 p.m. to 5:00 p.m.

- "Good Evening" → From 5:00 p.m. onward (6:00 p.m. for business), but some may wait until sunset to use it.

- "Good Night" → Used only as a farewell, not a greeting.

ELEVATORS, DOORS, AND CARS

ELEVATORS

1. When entering an elevator, wait for people to step out before you walk in.

2. If you are standing next to the panel, ask individuals what floor they want and press the button for them.

3. If you are already in the elevator, be sure to make room for people as they walk in.

4. Step aside to allow others to exit when they reach their floor.

DOORS

1. If a door is closed, knock and wait for a response before entering.

2. It's polite to hold the door open for people when entering or exiting doors.

3. Be sure to hold the door open for others if the door pulls out towards you.

4. If you are entering a building when someone is exiting, allow them to step out first and then you may enter afterward.

5. If an individual is about five steps behind you, hold the door for them and allow them to grasp the door before you let go.

6. With revolving doors, one person should enter at a time.

CARS, SUVS, AND TRUCKS

1. For women to remember when getting into a car, there are two ways to do this.
   - Method One – Sit first, then turn your legs inward to the car.
   - Method Two – Sit first, then turn your legs inward one at a time towards the car.

2. When exiting the car, there are two ways to get out.
   - Swing both legs outwards, then stand outside the car.
   - Swing one leg at a time, then stand outside the car.

3. How to properly get into an SUV or truck.
   - If a rail is present, use it. Step onto the rail with your back towards the seat of the car.

- It is okay to hang on to the door or handles.

- Keep your knees close together. Swing your legs into the vehicle one at a time or both at the same time.

4. In all instances, when getting in and out of vehicles, be mindful of how you move when you are wearing a dress or a skirt.

FOR MEN TO REMEMBER ABOUT CARS, SUVS, AND TRUCKS

1. If you are with your wife, sister, aunt, grandma, or female friend, hold the car door open for them.

2. Ladies are always first. Let the ladies enter the car first before you.

3. If the female is driving, open the driver's door for her, then get in on the passenger's side.

CHAPTER 4

Communication with Grace and Confidence

COMMUNICATION SKILLS: VOICE, VOCABULARY, AND TONE

The way we speak has much to do with the way we are perceived by others. A good way to establish a positive impression on others is to be mindful of what we say and the manner in which we speak.

Avoid speaking in a tone that sounds tired or depressed. Don't speak too loudly or too softly. Choose an even pleasant tone of voice. Mind your tone of voice when you are speaking to people in the service industry, such as a grocery clerk, barista, waiter or waitress, bus driver, or flight attendant.

Avoid using slang language. Pronounce your words correctly. Don't grunt. Instead, simply say yes or no when answering a question.

Don't use the same words over and over. For example, avoid saying the word "like" multiple times. Instead, use the phrase "for example" or "for instance."

There are many ways to communicate through speech, and the way we use our voice can completely change the meaning of what we say. By putting stress on different words, adjusting our tone, or changing our pitch, we can convey emotions, emphasis, or even our stance on a situation. For example, a simple phrase can sound ordinary on the surface, but the way it is spoken can reveal much more about our thoughts or intentions.

Consider the phrase, *"I'm not going to drive."* The meaning shifts depending on which word is emphasized.

If I say, "**I'm** not going to drive," the emphasis suggests it's me who won't drive.

If I say, "I'm not **going** to drive," it may indicate hesitation or a change of plans.

If I say, "I'm not going to **drive**," it implies I won't drive, but I may still be involved in another way.

These subtle changes show how tone and emphasis shape communication.

UNDERSTANDING BODY LANGUAGE: PRESENCE, GESTURES, AND NONVERBAL CUES

WHAT YOUR STANCE CONVEYS

The way you carry yourself speaks volumes before you even say a word. Standing with your hands behind your back conveys grace and authority, while keeping them in your pockets can appear casual or indifferent. Avoid holding one arm at the elbow, as this can make you seem shy or insecure. Similarly, crossing your arms or ankles can give the impression that you are closed off or hesitant.

WHAT YOUR SITTING POSTURE SAYS

Your body language when seated also communicates confidence and attentiveness. Bouncing your knees up and down can make you appear nervous, while slouching may signal disinterest or laziness. Even the way you cross your legs can impact perception. Excessive leg crossing might make you seem defensive or closed off.

BALANCE IN BODY LANGUAGE

Moderation is key when using facial expressions and gestures. A smile can be welcoming, but overdoing it may come across as insincere. Maintaining eye contact is important, but too much can feel intense or intimidating. Hand gestures can enhance communication, but excessive movement may be distracting. Nodding is a useful tool to show agreement or understanding, but it should be natural and not overly exaggerated.

UNDERSTANDING PERSONAL SPACE

Body language also plays a crucial role in personal interactions. Imagine you are engaged in conversation, standing comfortably close to someone, and they suddenly take a step back. If you instinctively move forward and they step back again, they may have simply needed a bit more space. Recognizing these subtle cues is essential. Just because you feel at ease in close proximity does not mean the other person does. Paying attention to their movements can help you adjust accordingly and ensure the interaction remains comfortable.

THE POWER OF TOUCH IN HANDSHAKES

Physical contact, such as a handshake, also communicates unspoken messages. A traditional handshake is straightforward, but if someone places their hand on top of yours or touches your elbow during the handshake, it can indicate something beyond formality. In a professional setting, this might suggest authority or warmth. However, in a more personal context, a two-handed handshake with a gentle touch on the arm or elbow could signal attraction, connection, or a deeper sense of familiarity.

FACIAL EXPRESSIONS AND HIDDEN THOUGHTS

Facial expressions often reveal emotions even when we do not intend them to. A raised eyebrow, a subtle smirk, or a furrowed brow can convey disapproval or amusement before words are spoken. Some people have particularly expressive faces, making it difficult for them to hide their thoughts. For instance, someone reacting to an inappropriate comment might instinctively make a disapproving expression, even if they remain silent. Being aware of your own facial cues can help ensure your expressions align with the message you want to convey.

POSTURE AND PRESENCE IN PROFESSIONAL SETTINGS

Your posture affects how others perceive you and the level of confidence you project. Slouching or drooping shoulders may suggest uncertainty, while standing tall exudes confidence and readiness. Consider a restaurant server who constantly leans forward, hesitatingly asking, "Is everything okay?" This posture may unintentionally suggest that they are worried about bothering the guests.

Instead, standing upright and asking, "Would you like anything else?" with assurance commands respect and demonstrates a sense of ownership over their role.

Ultimately, body language is a powerful form of communication that influences how others perceive and respond to us. By being mindful of our stance, gestures, facial expressions, and posture, we can project confidence, professionalism, and approachability in any setting.

HAND GESTURES

There is nothing wrong with using our hands when we speak. There are some instances where we can use them to emphasize certain things. The key is to just keep it to a minimum so that it is not distracting.

If someone asks you a question, such as, "Where are the three such and such?" you can say, "Oh, well, the first one is here, the second one is there, and the third one is there." Your hand movements can help guide your response, adding a visual layer to your words and keeping you on track as you speak.

MODERN GENTLEMANLY AND LADYLIKE INTERACTIONS

It is a considerate gesture for a man to walk on the street side of the sidewalk when walking with a woman. This small act reflects awareness and thoughtfulness.

When going out on a date, if a man is picking a woman up from her home, he should meet her at her door.

He shouldn't honk the car horn or send a text message to alert his presence. When they return from the date, he should walk her back to the door. It is a respectful way to close the date.

Whenever in the presence of a woman, a man should always offer to help carry large packages or bags in order to assist her. The woman should always be gracious and say thank you.

Both men and women should avoid using profanity. Choosing gracious, respectful language in all situations strengthens your presence and preserves your credibility.

POLISHED AND COURTEOUS BEHAVIOR

When people ask you how you are, you should respond by saying: "I am well, thank you." Avoid one-word answers, such as "good" or "fine." It is always polite to follow up with an inquiry about the other person's well-being. So, ask them how they are. You can say, "How are you?"

Don't point. Use your open palm to direct a person to come and go. This small shift communicates respect, softens your message, and helps you appear more professional, polished, and inviting.

Don't get too close to people's personal space when standing next to them. This applies in places like grocery stores, bank lines, and coffee shops. Pay attention to body language. If someone leans away or shifts a bit, they may be signaling that you're too close. You can simply adjust your distance accordingly.

CHAPTER 5

Dressing the Part and Everyday Elegance

PERSONAL PRESENTATION AND FIRST IMPRESSIONS

Our appearance says a lot about us. People will make an assessment of you based upon the way you dress. And they will do it within seconds of meeting you. More importantly, the way we show up in the world physically and the clothing choices we make, have a lot to do with how we feel about ourselves and what we want to convey.

Your attire doesn't have to be expensive, it just needs to be neat, fitting, and appropriate for the occasion. As a matter of fact, it's even best to not lean into so many trends. My recommendation is that your wardrobe be heavy with smart, stylish and timeless pieces, and then you can have some trendy fun things mixed in.

There's plenty of room for self-expression when it comes to attire. You can show up in bold patterns, bright jewelry, a bow tie, or extravagant shoes.

Choosing an outfit with texture is another fun, creative way to show up. Go all out with sophisticated bling and a vibrant dress to express yourself. The key is to wear what suits you best and not give in to copying other people.

When you feel good about what you're wearing, it shows. You gain confidence. Your posture improves, and your overall energy becomes more open and polished. Dressing well isn't about being fancy, it's about being prepared, respectful, and aware of how your presence influences the space around you.

> ### THE FINISHING TOUCH
>
> A brooch should be worn on the left side of your outfit. Your watch belongs on your left wrist, with the face of the watch facing outward.

DRESSING FOR DIFFERENT OCCASIONS

What you wear to a particular event says a lot about your understanding of social norms. Whether you're attending a business event, a wedding, or a formal gathering, it's important for you to dress in a way that reflects that you understand the tone of the occasion. It also shows respect for the host and your fellow guests.

So, understanding the dress code, when it is stated, is key. For example, if an invitation says business formal, cocktail attire, or black tie optional, simply do your best to research and determine what is correct. (You can follow the guide that I have listed at the end of this chapter.) Make sure that you're in alignment with the dress code, most especially if you are in a high profile, meaningful, or leadership position. As you are selecting what to wear, if you are not absolutely sure, I recommend that you err on the side of dressing a notch up. It is better to be slightly overdressed as opposed to being underdressed whenever you show up to a particular event.

One other thing you want to make sure that you think about is when you're attending events that involve different cultures or customs, or if you're traveling, your attire matters. In a variety of regions, everything from formality to modesty to colors might seem acceptable in one instance, but in another, it might be deemed inappropriate. So doing your research in advance is important.

BUSINESS MEETINGS, CONFERENCES, AND CONVENTIONS

Choose professional, well-made pieces. For women, that could be a pantsuit, blouse and skirt, or a sheath dress with a blazer. For men, a suit and tie or dress slacks with a button-down and jacket. Neat grooming and polished shoes are a must. When attending conferences, polo style shirts and khaki pants are acceptable. For women attending conferences, tennis shoes, flats, and wedges are acceptable. Gone are the days when women had to suffer in high heels. Comfort is paramount.

JOB INTERVIEWS

It is a good idea to dress one level above what's expected in the everyday role. If it's a casual office, go business casual. If it's corporate, go business formal. Keep colors neutral and accessories minimal. Let your confidence, not your outfit be the boldest thing in the room.

If you have a very stylish or quirky style, dial it back slightly in this instance and use color or a single statement piece to show off your personality.

Although you want people to get to know you for who you are, you don't want to go all out yet, so that now the focus is on what you're wearing and not on your abilities.

WEDDINGS

The time of day and the location matter. For afternoon or outdoor weddings, a flowy dress or lightweight suit works well. For evening weddings, opt for cocktail or semi-formal attire. Unless the invitation states otherwise (for example, with destination weddings), avoid wearing white. The tradition still stands—that color is left to the bride.

RELIGIOUS SERVICES OR CEREMONIES

Modesty and respect are key. Dresses and skirts should hit just near the knee or below. Your shoulders should be covered. Men should wear slacks and a button-down or a jacket. If head coverings are customary, honor the tradition, whether or not you share the faith.

FUNERALS OR MEMORIAL SERVICES

Subdued colors have been the tradition for this occasion. This included black, navy, and gray. Accessories and makeup have traditionally been minimal. These sorts of occasions have evolved over time. Now, you might find the invitation will ask guests to wear a color that honors the deceased. People have gotten creative with accessories: bright ties, bold flowers or corsages, even choosing a certain type of sneaker to wear has changed. The key is to just make sure that you're in step with the recommendations or the request of the family.

If you're ever not sure what to wear, dress with moderation in mind. Your attire should reflect the tone of the gathering: respectful, not distracting.

COCKTAIL PARTIES

Opt for a sleek look that's dressy but not overdone. A little black dress, jumpsuit, or dressy separates work well for women. Men can wear dress slacks, a button-down shirt, and a blazer. Wearing a tie is optional unless specified.

FORMAL EVENTS (GALAS, FUNDRAISERS, ETC.)

This is your moment to really get fancy! Think long gowns, elevated accessories, and classic elegance for women. For men, a tuxedo, or formal dark suit with a tie or bow tie is appropriate. Go for timeless attire over trendy styles that can feel out of place.

DINNER AT SOMEONE'S HOME

Aim for elevated casual. A nice blouse and pants, a sweater dress, or a polished top with dark jeans works well. Athleisure wear is a good choice too. You want to look like you made an effort but not like you're trying to outdo your host. For men, try a crisp shirt, knit polo, or lightweight sweater with casual trousers or well-fitted jeans.

TATTOOS AND PIERCINGS

Just like clothing and accessories, body art is a personal choice that still calls for awareness and respect for the space you're in. Tattoos and piercings are more widely accepted than ever before, but etiquette is still about reading the room. In formal or professional settings, it's wise to be mindful of how and where your body art or piercings are displayed. You don't have to hide who you are, just use discretion when needed and consider the environment you're in.

WEARING WHITE BEFORE MEMORIAL DAY AND AFTER LABOR DAY

Back in the late 1800s, people would wear white during the height of the summer season, starting from Memorial Day through Labor Day. Afterward, folks would shift to colors and fabrics that reflected the fall season. It was also during this time that the color white became closely associated with individuals in the more affluent part of society. Somehow, this notion of not wearing white after Labor Day ended up becoming known as an etiquette standard and fashion faux pas.

Today, this is not the truth. It is perfectly fine to wear white all year long. Whether you're on the West Coast in California, the Southeast in Florida, or any part of our nation, you can confidently wear your white. The shade you choose, whether bright white, winter white, or eggshell, including your shoes, depends entirely on the ensemble you pull together for your own fashionable look.

UNDERSTANDING COMMON DRESS CODES

Understanding the requested dress code at different events can take a lot of guesswork and stress out of getting ready. If you've been invited to an event that is annual or repeated, go online and take a look at photos to see what people wore before. This will give you a great visual of what might be expected at the event. Oftentimes, the invitation itself will indicate the dress code, offering helpful guidance on what to wear. There are basic categories for attire such as casual, cocktail, or formal. Keep in mind that some hosts like to get creative with wording. Dress codes with fun or unusual names, like "Coastal Cocktail," typically still follow traditional attire guidelines.

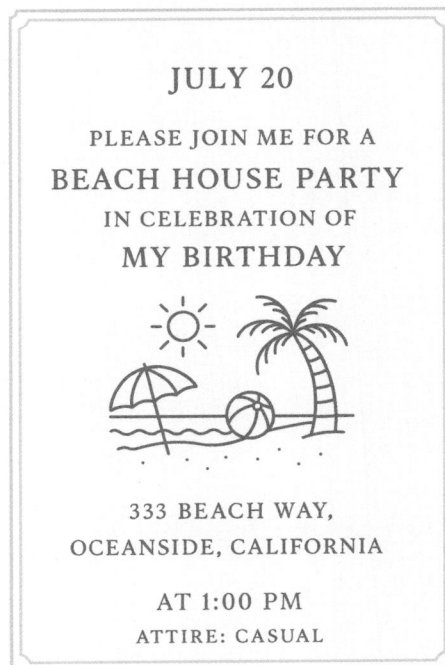

JULY 20

PLEASE JOIN ME FOR A
BEACH HOUSE PARTY
IN CELEBRATION OF
MY BIRTHDAY

333 BEACH WAY,
OCEANSIDE, CALIFORNIA

AT 1:00 PM
ATTIRE: CASUAL

COMMON DRESS CODES AND WHAT THEY TYPICALLY MEAN

Dress Code	What it Means	Example
CASUAL	*Relaxed everyday wear*	**Women:** Sundress with flat sandals and a woven tote. Easy, breezy fabrics like cotton, jersey, or linen **Men:** Jeans or shorts with a polo or T-shirt and sneakers or loafers.
SMART CASUAL	*Casual but a little more polished*	**Women:** Dark jeans, simple T-shirt, structured blazer, and clean sneakers or loafers. Effortless polish with a relaxed foundation. **Men:** Dark jeans or chinos with a polo or casual button-down. Optional blazer, loafers or clean sneakers.
BUSINESS CASUAL	*Office appropriate but not formal*	**Women:** Cardigan over a blouse, dark jeans or trousers, heeled ankle boots, and a structured tote. **Men:** Dress slacks with a button-down or sweater. Optional blazer, leather shoes.
BUSINESS FORMAL	*Traditional professional attire*	**Women:** Knee-length sheath dress or slacks with a blouse. Closed-toe pumps, minimal accessories, structured handbag. **Men:** Dark suit and tie, dress shirt, polished oxfords.
COCKTAIL	*Dressy usually for the evening*	**Women:** Sleek cocktail dress or a formal jumpsuit. Strappy heels, statement earrings, evening clutch. **Men:** Suit without a tie. Crisp shirt, dress shoes.
SEMI-FORMAL	*Elegant but not fully formal*	**Women:** Elegant dress—long or tea-length, often with a slit or draping. Dressy heels and jewelry. **Men:** Dark suit and tie. White or light dress shirt, leather shoes.
BLACK TIE	*Very formal evening wear*	**Women:** Floor-length gown with formal detailing. Sparkling accessories, clutch, heels. **Men:** Black tuxedo, white dress shirt, black bow tie, patent leather shoes.
WHITE TIE	*The most formal of all dress codes*	**For women:** floor-length gown, gloves are traditional, elegant updo, refined jewelry, classic heels. **Men:** Black tailcoat, white waistcoat and bow tie, formal shirt with studs, white gloves optional.

CASUAL   SMART
CASUAL

BUSINESS
CASUAL   BUSINESS
FORMAL

COCKTAIL   SEMI-
FORMAL

BLACK
TIE   WHITE
TIE

PART TWO

Social Graces and Public Etiquette

NAVIGATING PUBLIC LIFE
WITH ELEGANCE AND EASE

Public grace isn't about perfection. It's about showing respect, patience, and care in every shared space we occupy.

- ELAINE SWANN -

CHAPTER 6

Thank-You Notes, Gifts, and Thoughtful Responses

Public grace isn't about perfection; it's about showing respect, patience, and care in every shared space we occupy. Navigating public life with poise and purpose requires us to do more than just follow a set of rules; it's about being mindful of others and doing so in real time. Whether you are returning an item at a store, working out at the gym, or cheering at a game, etiquette provides the mindset for being gracious, even in very casual or chaotic environments. These chapters will help you master those small moments that define our social fabric. Because wherever you go, whether it's the coffee shop, the parking lot, or the airport, your presence is going to leave a mark. Let that mark be a kind one.

THANK-YOU NOTES

The purpose of writing a thank-you note is to show your gratitude towards an individual because of their generosity or kindness towards you. The handwritten thank-you note is still the epitome of social-savvy style.

You can create a basic thank-you station that contains cards, pens, stickers, and stamps. Always have a set of stylish note cards, thank-you cards, and special occasion cards on hand.

- Thank-you notes should be written within one week.

- A good practice is to try to write the note within three days of receiving the gift.

- After a large event such as a wedding where a honeymoon is taken afterward, it is acceptable to send notes upon your return.

- With bereavement, the time frame is relaxed, and notes are sent when the sender is emotionally ready to do so.

- Always sign your notes, letters, and postcards with your first and last name.

- If it is addressed to a relative, you may use your first name only.

- If you're invited to spend several days at a friend's house, it's a nice gesture to write a thank-you note to your host afterward.

- If you have a large party and you receive a great number of gifts, it is still important for you to write handwritten thank-you notes.

- Do not print your notes—instead, take your time and write them a few at a time.

SENDING THANK-YOU NOTES

SENDING THE NOTE

The person who received the gift should write the note. Group notes should be reserved for receiving a group gift. For example, if a gift is received for your entire household, it's alright to send one card—just ask each recipient to sign.

TIMELINE FOR THANK-YOU NOTES

In order to avoid prolonging your thank-you, it's a good practice to write your notes as soon as possible. If you feel you're late, send the note anyway: a late note is always better than no note at all.

HOW TO WRITE A THANK-YOU NOTE

1. Write the person's name.

2. Say the words "thank you."

3. Name the gift.

4. Say something about the gift they gave you.

5. You can say what you like about it.

6. Or, you can say what you will do with the gift.

7. Sign your name at the bottom of your note.

> *Dear Betty,*
>
> *Thank you for the beautiful crystal vase. It complements our home*
>
> *beautifully and we will enjoy placing flowers in it year-round.*
>
> *Warm regards,*
>
> *Jerry and Nina Swann*

THANK-YOU NOTES VIA EMAIL OR TEXT MESSAGE

It's important to recognize that email and texts do not transfer emotion well. A thank-you note should convey some sort of emotion.

There are a few instances when you should avoid sending a thank-you note via email or text message. They are:

- An elderly relative

- A dear friend

- An expensive or well-thought-out gift

- A very special gesture or occasion

Emailing or texting is just not as personal as a note written by hand. Additionally, they might view it as disrespectful or find it invaluable. It is alright if you send a quick text initially, but it is a good idea to follow up with a handwritten thank-you note. The really neat thing is that a handwritten note sent by mail has a 100% open rate and is still a great way to convey thanks. A written thank-you in these key instances is the best choice for sincerely expressing your gratitude.

THOUGHTFUL GIFT-GIVING TIPS

When a Gift is Not Required

If the invitation says "no gifts," respect the host's wishes. Your presence truly is the present at some events.

Group Gifting

It's perfectly acceptable (and thoughtful) to chip in on a group gift, especially for weddings, showers, or office celebrations.

Gift Cards Are Okay

When in doubt, a tasteful gift card to a favorite store, coffee shop, or online platform is always appreciated.

Late Gifts

If your gift is going to arrive late, that's okay, a thoughtful card explaining that it's on its way is a gracious move.

Arriving Empty-Handed

You're invited to an event like a baby shower, bridal shower, or birthday. You buy the gift online and schedule the delivery, but when the day arrives, you feel a little weird walking in empty-handed, right? Just bring a card with you. Your handwritten message adds a personal touch and shows your thoughtfulness until the gift arrives.

THOUGHTFUL RESPONSES – NAVIGATING DIFFICULT LIFE SITUATIONS WITH GRACE

THE DEATH OF A LOVED ONE

As with many families, the passing of a loved one can be very bittersweet. Bitter is the sense of loss and knowing the person won't be with us here in the flesh. Sweet is the love, laughter, and tender moments spent with family members near and far.

I lost my mother, Betty Lee, in 2017. During that time, I heard so many comments, some kind, some awkward. One thing I know for sure is that it can be hard to figure out what to say when someone loses a loved one. Here is some guidance to help you navigate those moments with care and confidence.

When you offer your condolences, keep in mind that less is more. Don't drone on and on or give a long-winded talk; just keep it simple and to the point. You are less likely to have a slip of the tongue and say something off-color.

Don't say: "Well, they lived a long life," or "It was God's will."

Do say: "My condolences to you and your family," or "I'm sorry for your loss.

Even though the individual may believe in God, tragedy is hard to put into perspective so soon. So, it's best to say something like, "I'm praying for you and your family."

When talking with the person, it is perfectly fine to reminisce about a special or light-hearted moment that can bring laughter. People tend to enjoy talking about good memories. It lifts their spirits.

When you offer help, do so by actually saying what you can do. Anything from picking up relatives from the airport to transporting flowers to the memorial service is a great way to assist. Here are some other ways to help:

- Offer to watch or tend to small children.

- Taking older children out for a short while to give the family a break.

- Tidy up their house (ask first—people can be territorial during troubling times).

- Run simple errands.

- Bring supplies such as food, beverages, and paper products. (Paper towels and toilet paper are some of the first items to go when you have a lot of people in the house.)

WHAT TO SAY WHEN

Have you ever been in a situation where you've said something and regretted it later? Once spoken aloud, your words become both a part of your personal history and a part of other people's memories. Remember that our words cannot be taken back, so release them with care.

Think twice before you speak and pay close attention to what's coming out of your mouth. In difficult circumstances, you should take more time to listen than to talk.

If you go beyond a simple well-wish or condolence, keep it simple by offering practical advice. Don't be pushy, though. Just make it known and allow the individual to decide if they want to actually use it.

SOMEONE ANNOUNCES THEY'RE GETTING DIVORCED.

Don't say: "Well, that's okay, you're better off without him/her".

Do say: "I'm very sorry to hear that".

SOMEONE EXPERIENCES THE DEATH OF A LOVED ONE.

Don't say: "They're in a better place now".

Do say: "My condolences to you and your family".

SOMEONE (OR THEIR WIFE) HAS A MISCARRIAGE.

Don't say: "Maybe something was wrong with the baby, and that was God's way of handling it."

Do say: "I am very sorry to hear that. Please let me know if there is anything that I can do."

SOMEONE IS FIRED OR LAID OFF FROM THEIR JOB.

Don't say: "Maybe this means that you're going to find something better."

Do: Be sympathetic and give practical assistance, such as a recommendation or information about other job openings.

SOMEONE (OR A RELATIVE) IS SICK OR TERMINALLY ILL.

Don't: Ask too many questions. Don't speak of end-of-life or afterlife topics and subjects.

Do: Show sympathy by helping the person with managing their family or day-to-day responsibilities.

SOMEONE ANNOUNCES THEIR (OR THEIR WIFE'S) PREGNANCY/BIRTH.

Don't say: "Really, how old are you again?" Don't tell horror stories of pregnancy or birth challenges.

Do: Congratulate them and offer referrals for pediatricians, books, websites, mobile apps, etc.

SOMEONE GETS ENGAGED OR MARRIED.

Don't say: "Finally, I thought you two would never get married!" or "I know I'm invited"!

Do say: Congratulations, I wish you both the very best!

CHAPTER 7
Grace in Public:
From Returns to Customer Service

ETIQUETTE FOR RETAIL RETURNS

1. Wear your patience hat. Walk in the store prepared to wait. Wait in line, wait for an answer from a supervisor, and wait for the transaction to be completed. It's difficult to be polite and considerate of others when you are in a hurry because your mind is on other things. Just leave and come back. Timing is crucial to getting what you want.

2. Practice good gadget etiquette. Give your full attention to the sales clerk by staying off that cell phone. Remove both earphones if you're listening to music or a podcast on your phone.

3. Mind your body language. Flopping things down on the counter and pushing items around will get your mission stopped before you even get started.

4. Use tact when explaining why you are returning the item. Don't insult the store, the manufacturer, or the salesperson.

5. Respect is essential. The sales clerk may be younger than you, but it's still important to speak to them with respect. Use kind words and phrases: "Yes please," "No thank you, I'd rather not have a store credit," or "I wasn't aware of the restocking fee."

6. Be charming. Smile when you speak, call the person by their name, say something nice, and let them know you sympathize with how they may be feeling if the store is busy.

7. Watch your tone of voice. Saying, "I bought this for my husband, and he hated it" can take a bad turn, depending on how you say it.

8. Apply the relationship rules. Bite your tongue to get the job done, pick and choose your battles, and know when to walk away. Sometimes, it's just not worth the fight.

9. Don't make a scene. If you are told no, just politely say thank you, gather your things calmly, turn, and leave. You want to leave the door open to have your case heard by another employee, supervisor, or even the store manager. You'll hurt your future chances if you're labeled as "The lady who cussed Jane out over the pink slippers."

10. If you have to call later to speak to a manager, don't start off in a huff, complaining and blaming the staff. Use what I like to call your "radio voice." It's that smooth, calm tone of voice. It puts the other person at ease and conveys warmth. If you succeed in getting what you want, don't gloat when you return to the store.

11. If you just cut your losses and keep the item, try your best to adjust your mindset. You can re-gift it, sell it online, or donate it to a resale store.

> ◆ EXTRA TIDBITS ON MAKING RETURNS
>
> Be prepared to make the transaction a swift and smooth one.
>
> Find out the return policy in advance.
>
> Have the original packaging, if possible.
>
> Have tags on hand, even if they are not attached.
>
> Have your receipt, if at all possible.

RESPECT IN ACTION: GRACE IN PUBLIC PLACES

POLITENESS WHILE TRAVELING

Gate Agent

Don't rush to the podium the moment the agent arrives. Their first few moments are spent logging in and getting flight information. Stand back from the podium and wait until you are called. Mind your body language; flopping your luggage down, flailing your hands, or leaning over the counter to look at the computer screen will get your mission stopped before you even get started.

Flight Attendant

Establish the fact that you are a good traveler early on. Greet the flight attendant with a smile and a pleasant "hello" at the door of the plane and any others as you are walking down the aisle.

Respect is essential. Use kind words and phrases. Say "please" and "thank you." Be sure to keep your requests reasonable. Treat them with decency and respect, and you'll find they're more willing to help you out if you need a favor.

KINDNESS DURING YOUR HOTEL STAY

Front Desk Clerk

Always use the person's name. Just glance at the name tag. This will help to establish a friendly rapport and make your exchange with them more personable.

Housekeeping

Your very first interaction should set the tone for your stay. Introduce yourself. Ask for their name. Strike up a very brief yet pleasant conversation. When you see them in the hall, greet them with a simple "hello" or "good morning." Use their name if you are able to spot a name tag. It is more likely that they'll remember your kindness when you need something later.

KINDNESS IN BEAUTY AND WELLNESS SPACES

SALON, SPA, AND NAIL SERVICES

Be considerate of their time. Always arrive on time for your appointment. Call well enough in advance if you are going to be late or must cancel.

Hate the outcome? If you have a problem with the results of your service, address your concerns in private or over the telephone. Try not to become overly emotional and stick to your case. Say something like, "Susan, I appreciate your hard work, but my hair color is nothing like what I expected. Is there anything we can do to correct it?"

Factor in a tip with every service. Being a steady client and fair tipper will set the stage for superior service.

COURTESY TOWARD RESTAURANT STAFF

Have to send food back? Only do so if it's not what you ordered, not prepared correctly, tastes spoiled, or has a hair or pest in it. Speak calmly and discreetly to the server when making your request.

COURTEOUS BANKING INTERACTIONS

It's important to be patient during the busiest times of the day. This would include lunch hours or on Fridays. It is not unusual for the bank to have a line during these times.

Once a teller is finished with a prior customer, instead of rushing to their window, wait just a moment and allow them to call you up to the counter. Oftentimes, they may need to finish up a transaction before beginning to work with the next customer.

Avoid using your phone at the counter unless it has something to do with your transaction. This small act of courtesy shows that you have respect for the person who's helping you.

Prior to going to the counter, be organized. Have your bank card, your ID, any paperwork, or accounting details ready to go. Your banker will appreciate this, and it will make your transaction go smoothly.

THOUGHTFUL INTERACTIONS WHILE SHOPPING

RETAIL STAFF AND STORE ASSOCIATES

While you're in the store, acknowledge the presence of the clerk with a simple hello. Even if you are just browsing, having a little warmth at the beginning of your shopping experience can make a big difference.

If you need help finding a specific size or item, or if you have a question, use kind and courteous language such as, "Would you mind helping me find...?" or "Could you point me to ...?" Associates will appreciate your polite approach.

Be respectful of the store space. Don't leave things in a pile or drop them off in areas where they don't belong. Don't open any products without first asking for assistance.

When you check in or out, if you can, use the associate's name. This will make your thank-you sound more genuine, which can really have a big impact.

REMEMBER: SERVICE PROS ARE PEOPLE TOO

- Think before you react.

- In conflict, attempt resolution, then let the manager do the managing.

- Nail Technicians – Avoid talking on your cell phone, try talking to the technician more.

- Parking Valets – Remember to keep cash on hand so you can leave a tip.

- Food Servers – Check the restaurant's policy for large parties before you go.

- Flight Attendants – Just follow the airline rules.

- Sales Associates – Be sure your transactions are hand to hand.

CHAPTER 8

Polite in Public Fitness, Fun, and Famous Faces

SWEATIQUETTE – USING PROPER ETIQUETTE AT THE GYM

Avoid overly loud grunting. Your loud noises, and overzealous grunting, can be distracting to club members around you.

Wipe up your sweat from the exercise equipment. Research has shown that people have contracted communicable diseases such as rashes and ringworm from bacteria on exercise equipment. Be kind, and take a moment to protect yourself as well as others, by simply wiping the equipment.

Return equipment to its proper place and/or back to the low setting. Just take a couple of extra steps to leave things organized for the next person. If you take out free weights, put them back. If there are various settings on the equipment you're using, be courteous and reset the machine to its lowest setting.

Don't overdo it with the camera. It's not unusual to show the world what we're doing through our social media channels. It can be motivating and inspiring to others. However, don't overdo it by turning your session into a feature film set. Filming your workout session should not be a distraction to others, nor should it physically get in the way of people trying to work out. Don't interrupt people to ask them to film you. Don't set up your phone in a space that might be in the way of someone else. The key here is to get the shot and be done with it.

Think about how you smell. Even though you're going to perspire when working out, don't wear the same sweaty clothes over and over again. Using deodorant and wearing laundered clothes will help prevent natural body order from becoming so strong it offends the people around you.

Avoid staring at people. Keep in mind that most individuals are at the gym not only to maintain a healthy body but to work on problem areas as well. This means people, women especially, may be feeling somewhat uncomfortable just being there. Don't make matters worse by staring.

Don't hog the machines. It's important that you pay attention to the people around you so that you are mindful of how long you are using each machine. This includes the cardio machines as well. If you've signed up to use specific equipment for a given time, be sure you stick to it as a courtesy to others.

Keep the gym and locker room clean. The staff at your gym are not there to follow behind and pick up after you. Take your water bottles, towels, etc. with you when you leave the club. And don't forget to clear the area around your locker of your personal belongings.

Keep conversation brief or move to another area to talk. There are times when you may find yourself in conversation with an acquaintance or meet someone new. People are there to concentrate on their work out, and your voice may be a distraction. If you see your conversation is going to be prolonged, then step into another area, such as the lobby, so you don't disturb people nearby.

Follow the club rules. Rules may vary from club to club for different reasons, depending on the management. Don't take them personally because every member is expected to follow them. You'll have a better workout experience and make your life simple by following the posted guidelines.

SPA ETIQUETTE

CREATE A PEACEFUL EXPERIENCE

A spa visit is meant to be a time of relaxation and renewal. Speak softly throughout the space, as others are there to unwind and enjoy their treatments.

CELL PHONE COURTESY

To maintain a calm and distraction-free environment, turn off or silence cell phones once inside the spa. Many spas do not permit phone use beyond the reception area, so it's best to keep devices tucked away.

CANCELLATIONS

If plans change, most spas require at least twelve hours' notice for cancellations or appointment changes. Canceling with less notice may result in being charged in full.

WHAT TO WEAR

Most spas provide robes, slippers, and personal lockers for guests. If planning to use a co-ed steam room, bringing a bathing suit is a good idea. When leaving, wear something comfortable to slip into.

HEALTH CONSIDERATIONS

Before booking a service, inform the spa of any medical conditions or special needs. Those who are pregnant or have high blood pressure should avoid heat treatments. Certain skincare and waxing services also have restrictions related to pregnancy and prescription medications, so checking ahead is important.

GRATUITIES

Tipping is always at the guest's discretion. Gratuities are not typically included in the cost of spa services or gift certificates, but if guidance is needed, the spa concierge can offer recommendations.

RETURNS AND GIFT CERTIFICATES

For product returns, refunds are often available within a specific set of days with a receipt. Without a receipt, some spas may offer boutique credit instead.

TAMING THE SHOPZILLA: POLITENESS ON ERRANDS

Set boundaries for your children and teens before you leave the house. Make it clear beforehand that there will be no running around the store and that your child should not touch or play with any of the items in the store. If you allow your teen to shop alone, be sure you have set a time and place to meet back together.

Make sure small children are well rested and fed before you go. This will prevent you from having to deal with embarrassing temper tantrums.

Make sure you are well rested and fed before you go. This way, you'll avoid throwing any temper tantrums of your own as well as having a short fuse while shopping.

Avoid blocking the aisles with your cart or stroller. Be mindful of people around you. Try to follow the same type of rules you would on the road, by allowing people to pass and get by.

Speak to the clerks and employees of the store with courtesy and kindness. During the holidays, stores are crowded, and the staff is doing their best to be kind to everyone. Don't make it any harder on them than it needs to be. A bright smile and a cheery hello can do wonders.

Don't grab at items while other shoppers are looking at them. Shopping is not a rugby match. Sure, you want to get to those sale items first, but don't make a spectacle of yourself in doing so.

Refrain from making nasty remarks about other customers, the store staff, and goods in the store.

If you witness someone behaving badly in public, they more than likely couldn't care less what your opinion of them is, so keep yours to yourself. Also, if you don't like the merchandise at the store you're in, leave and go to another store.

Don't push or crowd at sale tables or the checkout counter. You never know what little thing can set another person off, so to avoid any possible ugly confrontation, play nice!

Avoid prolonged cell phone conversations while shopping. Try not to walk around the store chatting on your phone a mile a minute. It's easier to pay attention to your surroundings if you're not on your phone too long. Distracted shoppers are a prime target for pickpockets and package thieves.

You should never ask or expect a clerk waiting upon a customer to leave that person and attend to you. Wait patiently for your turn.

Don't get annoyed with the sales clerk for doing their job, i.e., check/credit card approval or ID verification. No, the clerk is not picking on you personally. Specific rules are required by each store individually, so don't get all bent out of shape if one store checks your information and the other doesn't.

Never talk on your cell phone while at the checkout counter. Just tell the other party that you'll call them back after you've finished your transaction.

Hand your payment to the cashier rather than putting it on the counter. Your transaction is being done by a real human being, so be kind and use eye-to-eye and hand-to-hand contact. Your clerk will appreciate it!

FAMOUS ENCOUNTERS: POLITE APPROACHES TO CELEBRITIES

When you see a celebrity and want to approach, it is important to treat them in a manner that is respectable. Remember that you are a stranger to them and, even though you are familiar with their television or film character, you do not know them on a personal level. Keeping this truth in mind, here are a few things you should do upon coming into contact with your favorite celebrity.

Always address them by their last name. This is most proper when you do not know someone personally. For example, if you see Viola Davis you would say, "Hello Ms. Davis." If you see Denzel Washington you would say, "Hello Mr. Washington." Before you actually approach them, it's important to pay attention to their body language, as that will tell you whether they are approachable at the particular moment. Sometimes celebrities are with family, close friends, or in the middle of a business meeting and, hence, not available for pictures and autographs.

If you want a photo, ask permission first. You can say, "May I take a photo with you?" If you want an autograph, ask them, "May I have your autograph?" If you want a selfie, be very specific and tell them that's what you want. Some celebrities have stated that they feel selfies are very intrusive because they require space invasion for a good picture. If the celebrity declines a photo or autograph, simply place the occurrence in your memory book. Do not be mean or say anything inappropriate under your breath. Remember that these are individuals with full lives beyond the spotlight.

Be ready. If you are asking for an autograph, make sure you have pen and paper in hand so that you can make it swift. The same thing applies with a photo. If you're doing a selfie, have the camera turned and ready to go. If it is a photo where someone is taking the picture, make sure your designated photographer is standing, poised and ready with the camera. Preparation keeps you from taking up a tremendous amount of a celebrity's time.

Thank them. Make sure you give them a heartfelt thank-you. Look them in the eye when you speak. There is nothing ruder than taking a picture with someone and, as soon as the picture is done, walking away with your head buried in your camera without acknowledging the person. Even if a celebrity is surrounded by other people and someone else has come for an autograph or photo, it's still important for you to acknowledge and thank them. If they do have a moment, then say something nice to them. Perhaps you can say, "I really enjoy your work," or "I really enjoyed your last film."

CHAPTER 9

Polite in Public: Game Days, Gatherings, and Good Citizenship

GOOD SPORTS BEHAVIOR FOR PARENTS

Don't force your child to play. If your child is suffering from pain or injury or they just plain ol' dislike the game, don't force them to play. Organized sports are meant to help children develop respect, responsibility, fairness, and good social skills while having fun. There are several other activities your child can participate in to gain the same discipline.

Set positive examples for your child to see. This means your child needs to see you being courteous towards the coaches, parents, and other players. Set an example by offering kind words to the coaches, fellow parents, and players.

Avoid shouting directions. Instead, shout words of encouragement. Unless you are one of the official coaches, you should not be shouting out directions to your child or any others. Allow the coaches to do their job.

Address any concerns with coaches or officials privately. Don't even think about approaching the field or any officials in front of the players or other parents. If you are upset and have a serious concern, wait until you have calmed down and choose a time and place that is out of earshot of others.

Act as a troubleshooter for potential problem parents. If you see trouble brewing, let someone in charge know. Don't try to rule an unruly parent; you might just be adding fuel to the fire. As difficult as it may be, try to avoid confrontation at all costs and allow the sports officials to deal with problem parents.

GAME-DAY ETIQUETTE

Don't bring your parking lot frustrations into the game.

Don't be an annoyance to others by arriving late.

Don't be the "ballpark jerk."

An open seat does not mean "sit here."

Make it fun. Wear something that reps the home team.

Don't knock over children to catch a foul ball.

During the national anthem, stand, sing along, or remain quiet. Men should remove their hats.

If you're sitting in the family section, obey the family rules.

Mind your vocabulary, even if you are in the adult section.

Know your limit when it comes to drinking.

A DAY AT THE HORSE RACES OR POLO

ATTIRE

- Wardrobe should be an ensemble. Do not just slap a hat on because it's opening day.

- Choose colors and style that complement skin tone, rather than just picking a current trend.

- Pantyhose are still in vogue, and they look great with closed-toe shoes.

HATS

- Okay for ladies to wear indoors.

- Be mindful of the folks behind you.

- If you remove it, hold it in your left hand, interior facing inward.

GLOVES

- Remove them once you enter a building.

- Don't shake hands with them.

- Don't eat or drink with them.

- Hold your pocketbook and gloves in your left hand to shake with your right hand.

KISSING

- Don't greet strangers with a kiss.

- Tilt your head so you don't knock off other ladies' hats.

- Kisses are cheek to cheek.

HOLDING BEVERAGES

- Always hold by the stem, no matter what type of wine. This includes champagne.

- The teacup and saucer are both held, only if you are more than twelve inches from the table.

BEHAVIOR

- In the grandstand, remain seated until the horses have made the first turn of the track, then stand.

- No matter how exciting it gets, never stand on the seat itself.

- Be modest and good-natured when celebrating your win or loss.

- If you bet in line, don't hold up the line. Know who you are betting on beforehand.

GENERAL PUBLIC POLITENESS AND BEHAVIOR

PUBLIC POLITENESS

Public politeness is all about showing a little respect for yourself and others. It's quite simple to just be considerate of others. How does the saying go? "Do unto others as you would have them do unto you." Think before you speak or do—we'll all be better off.

LINE CRASHERS

Lines are everywhere, so just chill and be patient. Don't start any huffing and puffing. Don't breathe down folks' necks to get them to move forward quicker.

SMOKING/VAPING

Be conscious of which direction you blow your smoke. Always put cigarettes out in the proper place.

PARKING LOT BANDIT

Be courteous to other drivers in the parking lot. There's no sense in having road rage in the parking lot. You'll just end up dragging that same attitude into the store and wind up having a horrible shopping experience. Just take your time and play it safe. Stealing is bad even when it's a parking spot. If you see another car's blinker, that means you need to find another spot.

VISITING AND SOCIAL GATHERINGS ETIQUETTE

SHOULD YOU KNOCK OR TEXT WHEN AT SOMEONE'S DOOR?

When you arrive at someone's house, the proper thing to do is either knock on the door or ring the doorbell. Texting instead of knocking is not the right approach. Knocking or ringing the doorbell is how you appropriately alert someone of your presence. You are already connected to the person, and this is the polite way to announce you've arrived. And if you're dating someone, don't just text from the car, you should come to the door to collect them and walk them back when you return.

FLAG ETIQUETTE AND OUR NATIONAL ANTHEM

It's important that you respect our country, our forefathers, and our freedom. As citizens of the United States, we live in one of the few societies where we have the right to express ourselves at any time and live life exactly the way we want to (within the limits of the law). Living in a country that values freedom is something to appreciate and uphold.

FLAG ETIQUETTE

Our national school system has mandated that all public schools and some public gatherings recite the Pledge of Allegiance daily. It's important that you respect and honor this practice.

When you say the Pledge of Allegiance:

- Stand up along with the audience in a timely manner.

- Stand up straight.

- Don't fidget or move around.

- Place your right hand over your heart.

- If your culture or religion does not permit you to do this, simply sit or stand silently.

OUR NATIONAL ANTHEM

During most sporting events and special occasions, the national anthem is played to honor our country. During this occasion, you should remain respectful of the occasion. When the music begins you should:

- Stand if you are sitting.

- Avoid fidgeting or moving around.

- Remove your ball cap if you're wearing one.

- You may sing along with the lyrics if you know the words.

- If your culture or religion does not permit you to do this, simply sit or stand silently.

- During both of these occasions, I encourage you to challenge yourself to take a moment to reflect on something about your country or culture that you're proud of.

PART THREE

Dining *Etiquette*

SAVORING EVERY MEAL WITH
STYLE AND SOPHISTICATION

Dining is not just about how you use your knife and fork at the table; it's a dance of consideration, tradition, and awareness of those at the table with you.

- ELAINE SWANN -

CHAPTER 10

Dining in the Digital Age

Dining is not just about how you use your knife and fork at the table, it's a dance of consideration, tradition, and awareness of those at the table with you. The table has long been a place where relationships are built, business deals are made, memories are created, and families are brought together. But even in the most informal setting, dining carries unspoken expectations. From the way you place your napkin on your lap to how you handle difficult foods, to offering a toast to someone, each gesture reflects a level of awareness and care. So, in this section, you will discover that dancing rhythm of proper dining—from setting the table to navigating around it successfully, to knowing what to order and what not to order when you're a guest. Whether you're at a backyard barbecue or a black-tie gala, you will be equipped to handle any meal with elegance and style.

THE EVOLUTION OF DINING ETIQUETTE

The etiquette for dining out has evolved in quite a unique way. Initially, dining out was very family-oriented or celebratory. It was a special occasion. Now, we have multiple groups of people coming together, but they're in their own little groups or ecosystems.

You've got spouses here, other groups of people there. The dining experience includes a lot of individuals, so things like splitting the check are very different now than before. Before, it was just a family group activity, the whole family went out to eat and came back home.

That's not the same anymore. You have families coming together and couples coming together, so the experience is different. With that, there are a lot of nuances—everything from splitting the bill to how you sit around the table.

We went from being very far removed, where it was boy-girl-boy-girl seating, to men sitting on one side of the table, to now embracing couples and saying, Sit next to your boo instead of all the men on one side and all the ladies on the other.

I don't want to bash men or anything like that because I've been happily married for more than twenty years, but that kind of machismo thing where the men only sit together has changed. Dining today is flexible; guests choose where to sit.

We laugh now when we see social media posts where they say, "Men want to know the tea too!" The experience has changed so much over the years, and it's great. But there are still nuances and guidelines we should follow so we can behave in a way that aligns with proper etiquette.

Etiquette is often about putting others at ease. The question becomes: How do we put people at ease when we are dining out, even among friends?

TABLE MANNERS AND MODERN ADAPTATIONS

As an etiquette professional, it's important for me to look at our world and what is important to people today instead of putting them in a box and saying, 'Do it this way.'

Some things are absolute rules. For example, you shake hands with your right hand. That's just the proper way to shake hands in Western society. But the notion of leaning on the table started because people felt it was too leisurely. Dining used to be very formal, so putting elbows on the table was viewed as lazy.

The reality is that putting your elbows on the table can cause a few problems, such as getting your clothing dirty, blocking someone else at the table, or hunching over, which doesn't look great.

Here's what's part of our new norm: If there is no food on the table and you're between courses or waiting for your food, it's acceptable to lean on the table and even place your elbows on it. You may lean in to engage in conversation, creating intimacy and connection.

PHONE USE AT THE TABLE

When you're dining at home, my recommendation is to avoid using your phone at all. When you're dining with your housemates, it's important to be connected to the individuals who are at the table. Mealtime at home is a time that should be sacred for connecting, fellowshipping, and making lasting memories.

Etiquette professionals used to say, 'Don't even bring your phone into the restaurant.' Now, we say, 'Don't forget your phone!' Make sure you bring it with you for a number of reasons. Phones are our personal assistants right in the palm of our hand. Restaurants use it to contact you when your table is ready. You may need to do research or contact someone else who's still on their way. We even use the flashlight on our phone to take a look at the menu.

Use your phone at the table only when it has something to do with the conversation at hand. If you're looking up an unfamiliar menu item, checking movie times, or finding parking info for someone joining you, that's fine.

Do not have text conversations with people who are not at the table or sit there scrolling through social media. It makes people feel disconnected. Again, etiquette is about putting others at ease.

TAKING PHOTOS WHILE AT THE DINING TABLE

It's acceptable to take photos of your food. Just don't do it during a job interview, in a professional setting, or during an intimate occasion where photo-taking can be a distraction.

Take pictures of your food, take pictures with your tablemates, and commemorate the moment. But wait until later to post those photos. Otherwise, you will end up being distracted by posting. You will find yourself cropping the photo, adjusting lighting, adding filters, writing captions, picking hashtags, and checking for comments. This will take time away from your tablemates, and you will miss the whole purpose of gathering together in fellowship.

CHAPTER 11

Modern Dining and Table Setting Essentials

TABLE SERVICE AND SETTINGS

- The entrée plate is placed directly in the center.

- Forks always go to the left of the plate.

- Knives always go to the right, directly next to the plate. Turn the sharp edges inward.

- The soup spoon goes to the right of the knife.

- Glasses are placed just above the knife and slightly to the right.

- Napkins can be placed in a variety of spots:
    - o In the center of the place setting, when a plate is not present.
    - o To the left of the forks.
    - o Underneath the forks.
    - o Folded decoratively and placed in the glass.

ADDITIONAL SETTINGS IN RESTAURANTS OR FORMAL DINNERS

- The charger (a large decorative platter) is placed in the center of your place setting.
    - o Before dining, the napkin may be placed in the center of the charger.
    - o The early courses such as soup and salad are placed on top of the charger.
    - o In some instances, the main course is placed on top of it, or it may be removed at this time.
    - o It is removed for dessert and coffee and tea service.
- Bread and butter plates are placed just above the forks and slightly to the left.
- The salad plate is placed to the left of the forks.
- A seafood or fish fork is placed to the left of the salad fork.
- A seafood or fish knife is placed to the right of the dinner knife.
- The dessert spoon and fork are set above the plate or are brought out with dessert.
    - o The handle of the fork faces the forks, and the handle of the spoon faces the spoon.
    - o The spoon is placed above the fork.
- The placement of utensils is dictated by the menu. The key is that you use utensils in an outside in fashion.
- The cup and saucer are placed just beside the spoon to the right. The handle of the cup should be turned towards the right.

ADDITIONAL BEVERAGE GLASSES WILL BE TO THE RIGHT OF THE WATER GLASS IN THE FOLLOWING ORDER:

- Water glass
- White wine glass
- Red wine glass
- Sherry glass (for a first course)
- Champagne flute (for an opening toast)

OTHER PLACE SETTINGS YOU MIGHT CONSIDER WHEN SETTING THE TABLE

SOUP ONLY

- The soup bowl is placed directly in the center.
- The liner, which is a small plate, is placed underneath the bowl.
- Your soup spoon goes to the right of the bowl.
- Glasses are placed just above the spoon and slightly to the right.
- Place the napkin to the left of your bowl.

TEA SETTING

- The appetizer/salad plate is placed directly in the center.
- The fork goes to the left of the plate.
- The knife goes to the right, directly next to the plate. Turn the sharp edge inward.
- The teaspoon goes to the right of the knife.
- The glass is placed just above the spoon and slightly to the right.
- The cup and saucer are placed just beside the spoon to the right. The handle of the cup should be turned towards the right.

THE PROPER WAY TO HOLD AND USE YOUR UTENSILS

The proper way to hold your cutlery is to pick up your fork and your knife at the same time. Hold your fork with the handle inside the palm of your hand and your index finger at the back of the fork. With your knife, the handle should also be in the palm of your hand, and your index finger at the back of your knife. When you cut, make sure that you are cutting on the backside of the fork. Do not cut underneath your fork and do not cut in between the tines. Also, be sure to hold your elbows in when you are cutting your food.

CUTTING AND EATING YOUR FOOD AMERICAN STYLE

- When cutting, hold the fork in your left hand with the tines down and hold the knife in your right hand.
- Place your knife at the top of your plate, with the blade facing you after cutting.
- Switch the fork to your right hand, place your left hand in your lap, and eat with the tines facing up.

CUTTING AND EATING YOUR FOOD CONTINENTAL (OR EUROPEAN) STYLE

- When cutting, hold the fork in your left hand with the tines down and hold the knife in your right hand.
- Pivot your left hand up towards your mouth and eat, keeping the tines of the fork down.

WHEN YOU ARE LEFT HOLDING YOUR KNIFE

There might be some instances when you are dining out and the server will take your plate away but encourage you to keep your knife. When this happens, you are not supposed to let the knife touch the table after you have been using it. You can place the knife on your bread-and-butter plate. If you don't have one, you can take your napkin and fold it slightly to create a little tent and then place your knife on top of it.

USING CHOPSTICKS

When using chopsticks, hold the top stick like a pencil and keep the bottom one steady between your thumb and ring finger. Only the top chopstick should move.

Don't point with your chopsticks, spear your food, or stick them upright in a bowl of rice, it's considered impolite. When you're not using them, rest them neatly on a chopstick holder or the edge of your plate.

SHARED UTENSILS

When dining family-style or at a buffet, always use the serving utensils provided to take food. Never use your personal utensils to serve yourself. Once food is on your plate, avoid reaching back in for more with your own fork or spoon.

HOW TO HOLD A WINE GLASS OR CHAMPAGNE GLASS

The proper way to hold a glass is by the stem, not at the bowl. This is because whatever's inside needs to stay at the proper temperature, whether it's chilled or room temperature.

Make sure that you do not put your pinky out. It came about when long ago the aristocrats wanted to show that they were better than other people, so they would put their pinky out. That is not the proper thing to do.

LIPSTICK, LIP GLOSS, AND YOUR GLASS

If you are wearing lipstick or lip gloss, sip from one part of the glass. This way, you won't have a ring of lipstick all the way around the glass. Rather than a ring, there will only be one discreet spot.

CHAPTER 12

Food-Specific Etiquette

HOW TO EAT BREAD (DINNER ROLLS) AND CROISSANTS

When eating bread, you are to break the bread into bite-sized pieces, placing a few on your plate at a time. Don't break up the entire roll. Then, take up one small piece at a time. Butter it and place it in your mouth. This method is still in step with proper etiquette at the dinner table. The term "breaking bread" comes from this custom. If you are eating a croissant, it is perfectly fine to pick up the croissant and use your fingers to pull it apart. It's bread that's made to unravel, so it will come apart easily. With both dinner rolls and croissants, don't saw either in half or slather them with butter like a piece of toast. When you break your roll or croissant into bite-sized pieces, it ensures that you're not overstuffing your mouth with food.

Croissants, specifically, are very delicate and get soggy very quickly, so don't dip them into your beverage. The soggy chunks might fall in, making things messy. There is no hard and fast rule that says you only add jam and jellies to your croissant. Although they are made with butter, you are free to add more if you like. How you enjoy it is a personal taste issue, not an etiquette issue.

EATING APPETIZERS

- Use the provided serving utensils and place them back where they belong.

- Do not pile too much food onto your plate. Take a few things and then return to the food service area to get more.

- No double-dipping. This means once you dip your food into a sauce or dressing and take a bite, do not dip into it a second time.

- If dipping sauce or dressing is served, be sure to place it onto your own personal plate and eat it from there.

- Do not stand over the food service area and eat. Move to another area to enjoy your food.

- If you attend a reception, you might not have a place to sit while you eat. This is intentional: the idea is for you to mix and mingle with the attendees who are present.

- When mingling with people at a reception, practice the following:
    - Keep your beverage in your left hand.
    - Leave your right hand available so that you may shake hands.
    - This will prevent you from offering a wet handshake because of the condensation on your glass.

- To hold a stemmed glass and an appetizer plate in one hand, do the following.
    - o Place the glass underneath the appetizer plate.
    - o Secure both with your right hand, keeping your left hand free to eat.

- Take food and beverage breaks. This means to maintain the following:
    - o Do not walk around holding your appetizer plate and beverage in both hands.
    - o Choose to eat first, then return for a beverage or vice versa.

- If tables are available, you may place your food and or beverage on a table.

- Once you have finished eating, follow one of these options:
    - o When a waste can is not present, place your napkin on top of your plate and push it toward the center of the table.
    - o When a waste can is not present, place your napkin on top of your plate and place it on a nearby waste station.
    - o When a waste can is present, gather your plate and any other items and place it in the receptacle. Do not toss it from a distance. Stand close so that you do not spill or splash.
    - o Do not place used plates or napkins near the food service area.

- When additional plates are provided, always return to the food service (buffet table) with a clean plate.

- When appetizers are hand-passed, take just one and use the napkin provided. If there's a sauce, dip only once. Be mindful not to reach across others or block the server. Simply take your item and step aside.

EATING VARIOUS FOODS
Vegetables and Fruits

Asparagus - Asparagus may be eaten with your fingers. Pick it up by the spear and use your fingers to eat it. If there is sauce on the asparagus or if it is limp, you may use your knife and fork to cut it.

Cherry Tomatoes - With cherry tomatoes, you would eat them just like grapes. Put the whole tomato on your mouth. Just be mindful and avoid squirting any of the juice from your mouth. If the cherry tomato is served in a salad, cut them just as you would your salad and eat with your knife and fork. If they're served as an appetizer, you may eat them with your fingers just as you would with grapes.

Crudités - Crudités are a variety of vegetables that are generally served with various dipping sauces. Be sure to place any sauce onto your own personal plate and eat it from there.

Grapes - It's fine to use your fingers to pick up the grapes. Just grab a small stem and place it on your plate. If no small stem is available, hold the main stem and pick a few grapes you'll eat yourself. Avoid touching grapes you won't take.

Fresh Fruit - Melons: If it is already cut into pieces or still on the rind, you can eat it with your fork and knife.

Meats and Proteins

Bacon - If the bacon is limp, cut it with a knife and fork. If it is crisp, you may pick it up and eat it with your fingers.

Barbecue - If you're in an informal environment, barbecue may be picked up and eaten with your fingers. If you're in a more formal setting, it's best to use a knife and fork.

Chicken Wings - Chicken wings are finger food. Whether they are fried or not, they're meant to be eaten with your fingers.

Crab and/or Lobster - When eating crab or lobster, use the hammer or cracking tool to crack the shell. You can also use your hands to crack it. Afterward, pull out the meat and eat it. Leave any parts of the crab/lobster that are inedible on the side of your plate. Keep in mind, soft shell crabs can be eaten with the shell and all.

Sushi - Sushi may be eaten with your fingers or chopsticks—both are acceptable. Use soy sauce sparingly by dipping the fish side (not the rice side) to avoid overpowering the flavor and making a mess. Eat sushi in one bite when possible, and avoid mixing wasabi into your soy sauce unless dining casually.

Shrimp - If shrimp is served with the tail on, hold it by the tail and eat the exposed portion in one bite. For shrimp cocktail, use the cocktail fork to dip and eat in one bite. If it's peeled with no tail, simply use your fork.

Oysters - Served on the half shell, oysters come with a small fork. Loosen the oyster, add lemon or sauce if desired, then tip the shell to your lips and slurp it in one motion. Swallow whole unless you prefer to chew.

Starches and Grains

Corn on the Cob - You can pick up corn on the cob with your hands and eat it neatly. Add salt, pepper, or butter on small sections as you eat the corn rather than sprinkling all over the entire ear of corn.

French Fries - You may eat French fries with your fingers; however, if they are served with an entree such as steak, you would eat them with a knife and fork.

Spaghetti - When spaghetti is served with a spoon, you can hold the fork in one hand and the spoon in the other hand, roll it until there aren't any strands dangling down. You may also cut the spaghetti with your fork and eat it. Another way is to take a few strands of spaghetti and spin them around a fork and eat it from there.

Tacos/Burritos - Any food with tortillas, such as tacos or burritos, can be eaten with your hands. If the tortilla is heavy and food might spill out or it is slathered with sauce, then use a fork and knife to eat it.

Oils and Accompaniments

Olive Oil - If you are served olive oil or balsamic vinegar with your bread, break it up into small pieces, pour a small amount of the oil or vinegar onto your own plate and eat it from there.

Olives - Olives can be eaten with your fingers. If it has a pit, eat the olive meat and then leave the pit.

Tapenades - Tapenade is a spread made from finely chopped olives, capers, and olive oil. You can spread it onto a small piece of bread using a knife, not by dipping, and eat it in one bite.

Appetizers and Finger Foods

Egg Rolls - It's perfectly fine to eat egg rolls with your fingers. If sweet and sour sauce is served, use the bowl or dish that is provided for you. Be sure not to double-dip if you're sharing the bowl with others.

Shrimp Cocktail - Use the tail as a handle. Dip once and eat in one bite. Don't double-dip in shared sauce.

Mini Meatballs or Skewers - Use the toothpick or skewer provided. Take only what you plan to eat.

Chips and Dip - Scoop chips and a spoonful of dip onto your own plate. No double-dipping in a shared bowl, even with a different side of the chip.

Cheese - Use the serving utensil or toothpick provided to place the cheese on your plate. Don't touch or hover over multiple pieces before choosing.

Crackers - Take up the crackers with your fingers only if no tongs or utensils are present. Be sure to take what you touch and avoid digging through the stack.

Charcuterie Meats - Use tongs or a serving fork to place slices on your plate. Try not to touch the meat with your hands or return any piece once picked up.

CHAPTER 13

A Proper Dining Experience: Start to Finish

YOUR NAPKIN

- Shortly after sitting down, your napkin is placed on your lap.

- Fold the napkin in half.

- The folded side of the napkin is placed towards your body, the open side away from you.

- The napkin is to be used to wipe food from your mouth during the entire meal.

- Use a small portion of the napkin to "dab" your mouth. Don't scrub as if using a washcloth.

- If you have to sneeze, cough, or burp, turn your head away from the table then sneeze, cough, or burp into your napkin.

- When burping, don't open your mouth too wide, and keep your lips closer together so the sound is not loud.

- Be sure to say, "Excuse me" after you have burped.

- If you have to leave the table, slightly fold your napkin and place it to the LEFT of your place setting. Be sure to put the napkin back on your lap once you have returned to the table.

MASK ETIQUETTE WHILE DINING

If you're wearing a mask while dining out, remove it completely once you're seated. It should be placed in one of three locations:

1. In your pocket

2. In your bag or purse

3. On your lap beneath your napkin

Do not hang it from one ear or leave it resting under your chin. You may put it back on between courses or when stepping away from the table.

EATING BREAD

- Place the bread on your bread-and-butter plate.

- Take the butter from the butter dish (sometimes it's wrapped) and place it on your bread-and-butter plate.

- If eating bread before any other course is served, you may move the plate directly in front of you.

- Once your meal has arrived and you are still eating your bread, move the plate to the left of you.

- Break off a small piece of bread, hold it in your fingers (not the palm of your hand) and butter it.

- Eat the buttered pieces of bread one at a time.

- Do not rub the butter on top of the bread or roll.

- Do not cut the bread in half and slather it with butter.

- You may sop up gravy with your bread but use your fork, not your fingers.

EATING SOUP

- Dip your spoon into the soup tilting it away from you, then lift the spoon into your mouth.

- Avoid hunching over the bowl and slurping.

- Sip the soup from the side.

- You may sip from the front end if meat, beans, or vegetables are present.

- It is permissible to pick up a soup cup that has handles.

- In between bites, you may rest your spoon inside the bowl.

- When finished eating your soup, place your spoon on the liner if one is present.

- At the end of your meal, place the spoon on the liner at the back of the bowl. If one is not present, then leave the spoon resting in the bowl.

EATING SALAD

- Be sure to use your salad fork and salad knife.

- Cut the large pieces of lettuce or vegetables and eat bite-sized portions.

- Don't cut the entire salad at once, cut sections at a time and eat in between.

SORBET TO CLEANSE YOUR PALATE

In a fine dining experience, you may be served a palate cleanser to consume. The purpose is to make sure the food flavors aren't blending together on your taste buds between courses. It is meant to provide a momentary respite from spicy or intensely flavored foods.

- The sorbet will be served in a stemmed glass or small bowl.

- Typically, it is a very small scoop. It is not meant to fill you up.

- Do not lift the glass.

- Hold the stem at the base between your third and fourth fingers.

- Use the dessert spoon unless one is brought out with the sorbet.

- Scoop up the sorbet and eat.

- Leave the spoon in the glass when finished.

EATING THE MAIN COURSE

- Be sure to use your dinner fork and your dinner knife.

- If you are having steak or pork chops, a separate steak knife will be brought out with your meal.

- Don't cut the entire entrée (or meat); cut bite-sized sections at a time.

EATING DESSERT

- Slide your dessert fork and spoon down from the top position to the left and right of your place setting.

- This is the signal that you are ready for dessert.

- Soft desserts such as custard or ice cream may be eaten with a spoon.

- Cake, pie, or crêpes being served à la mode (with ice cream) may be eaten with either the fork alone or together with the spoon.

DRINKING COFFEE AND TEA

- If you choose not to have coffee or tea, politely refuse the service. Do not turn your cup upside down.

- Allow the coffee or hot water to be poured into your cup.

- If you are having tea, open the tea bag and place it in the water.
  - Do not dip the bag up and down.
  - Simply allow it to steep to your desired likeness.
  - Lift the bag from the water and gently press it against the inside of your cup. This will relieve the bag of excess water.
  - Place the tea bag on the tea saucer.
  - With coffee and tea, add your condiments (milk, lemon, sugar) after it has been poured.
  - Place any packages or wrappers onto the saucer. If one is not present, make a neat pile on the table near you.

- o Do not stir in a circular motion. Instead, go back and forth in a twelve to six o'clock motion. This will prevent you from sloshing the liquid around and making a clicking noise with your spoon.

- o After stirring, place the spoon behind the cup onto the saucer. Do not drink your coffee or tea with the spoon in the cup.

- For teacups and demitasse cups (used for espresso), pinch your thumb and forefinger together around the handle. Do not loop your finger inside the handle.

- With coffee mugs, you may grasp the handle with all fingers.

- Do not hold your pinky out. Keep it tucked in.

TWO STORIES OF THE PINKY

1. When teacups were first made, they did not have handles. Tea drinkers would stick their pinky out to balance the cup while drinking.

2. In the early century, socialites and aristocrats adopted the idea of sticking their finger out while drinking to show a sign of high class. It did not work. The gesture is known as boorish and rude.

So, with that, do not hold your pinky out when sipping tea (or any beverage). It is not an etiquette thing.

At the end of certain stages of the meal, a small bowl will be placed before you along with a napkin. This is a finger bowl, and it is meant to clean your fingers. Follow these steps.

- The bowl will contain water along with lemon or flowers.

- Dip your fingers in one hand at a time.

- Rub your fingers together without splashing.

- Do not squeeze the lemon or flowers.

- Pat your hand dry with the napkin provided.

- Repeat with the opposite hand.

- Place the napkin to the left of the bowl when finished. The server will collect both.

SHARING FOOD FROM A PLATE

Sharing bites is common among close friends or couples, but it should always be done with care. If you'd like to offer someone a taste from your plate, use your clean fork or spoon to transfer the food to their plate, not directly to their mouth. Never reach over and eat directly from someone else's plate unless they offer and it's mutually comfortable. In formal settings or with people you don't know well, it's best to avoid plate-sharing altogether.

TOASTING ETIQUETTE

A toast is a known ritual where a drink is taken as an expression of honor, gratefulness, or goodwill towards another individual. Typically, positive words of expression accompany the drink and others join along.

WHEN YOU ARE DELIVERING A TOAST

- Stand.
- Hold your glass in your hand (does not matter which hand).
- If you do not know everyone in the room, introduce yourself. State your first and last name.
- Make a pleasant statement about the individual you are toasting.
- Be mindful about the amount of time you speak. Keep your statement minimal.
- At the end of your statement, raise your glass.
- End with a salutation:
    o "Salud!"
    o "Cheers"
    o "Here, here"
    o "Here's to (name)"

Example:

"Good evening, my name is Colton Gorham. I'd like to make a toast to Chloe Gorham. She has been a great help to our team and has displayed great leadership qualities. Thank you, Chloe, for helping us all achieve success. Here's to Chloe." (as you raise your glass).

WHEN YOU ARE THE INDIVIDUAL BEING TOASTED

- Remain seated.

- Do not raise your glass.

- Do not clap for yourself.

- Keep your hands in your lap.

- Smile pleasantly, make eye contact with the speaker, and say thank you.

CHAPTER 14

Fine Points of Dining Etiquette

WHERE TO PUT YOUR HANDBAG WHEN DINING OUT

There are a few places for you to put your bag when dining out. It does not go on top of the table because nothing goes on the table except for food.

You can set your handbag on the chair directly next to you if it's empty. Another option is to place it just behind you on your own chair. Simply scoot forward a bit and sit up nice and straight.

Depending on the purse and the environment, you may also hook it onto the back of your chair.

Some venues will bring out a little hook stand specifically for handbags. If they do, be sure to use it.

If you're carrying a clutch, you can place it on your lap with your napkin neatly resting on top. This keeps things elegant and out of the way.

Purse hooks that attach to the table are absolutely acceptable. Open the hook, place it on the table's edge, and hang your bag underneath. It's discreet and convenient.

The main thing to keep in mind is the type of bag you're carrying. It doesn't belong on the table or the floor. So, before you head out, make sure it's a bag that can rest on a chair, hang from a hook, or sit neatly on your lap.

GRACEFUL DINING AND HANDLING MISHAPS

If someone has food in their teeth, just discreetly tell them without making a spectacle of it. If you get food in your own teeth and can't swipe it away quickly with your tongue, politely excuse yourself from the table and remove the offending particle in the bathroom.

If you can't reach an item, ask the person nearest to you to pass it to you; don't reach over the person next to you. If you drop your silverware or napkin, pick it up if you're at home. At a restaurant, leave it and ask for another.

If you get a seed or bone in your mouth, remove it with your fork or with the thumb and forefinger of your left hand, and place it at the edge of your plate or bread and butter plate.

If you put something in your mouth and don't like the taste, do not spit it out. Don't try to hide behind your napkin to remove it. Simply chew the rest, swallow it, and leave the remainder on your plate.

Don't fumble around with empty packets from sugar, crackers, or other items. Simply place them under the rim of your plate, on your bread-and-butter plate, or on top of your saucer.

If you drop food or spill something, help clean it up. If you are dining out, call your server.

INTERACTIONS WITH OTHERS AT MEALTIME

BEING ESCORTED TO THE TABLE

Typically, the maître d' or hostess will escort a couple to their seats.

The general order would be the maître d' or hostess, followed by the woman and the man behind her.

If the maître d' or hostess does not assist the woman in sitting, the man should stop behind her and assist her.

WHEN SEATED AT THE TABLE

- The woman should sit facing the table, and the man should assist her in pushing her seat in while not actually pushing her in towards the table.
- When dining, if the woman stands up to leave the table, the man should stand as well.
- Once the woman returns to the table, the man should stand and assist her with sitting. Once she is comfortably seated, he may sit down.

ALCOHOLIC BEVERAGES

- If someone offers you a drink and you don't drink at all or choose not to engage at that moment, be gracious when you decline the offer.

- You may ask for an alternative. An option might be sparkling water or cranberry juice with a lime.

- Don't tell sordid stories about your personal history and why you don't wish to drink. This sort of conversation can make others feel uncomfortable.

GETTING THE ATTENTION OF YOUR SERVER OR HOST

- Lift your hand discreetly while attempting to make eye contact.

- Do not snap your fingers or wave frantically.

PAYING FOR THE CHECK

- When invited out to eat, the person who does the inviting pays.

- When dining with friends, family members, or an acquaintance, verify in advance whether you will share the cost of the meal.

- You can simply say, "Today, I'm treating you to lunch," or "Let's meet up and split dinner tonight."

- When dining in a large group, be prepared to add a bit of extra money to cover the cost of the gratuity.

- When dining with a large group, find out in advance if the diners expect to split the entire cost of the meal evenly.

o   This is a standard that many individuals have adopted recently.

o   It is only acceptable when the dining experience is elevated. An example would be a private dining room or an exclusive section of the restaurant.

o   In this instance, the experience is the focal point and not the meal.

- The proper thing to do is to adhere to the common standard set by the group.

- If you are ever not sure, then ask, "Say, how are we splitting the check today?"

CHAPTER 15

Final Touches: Mindful Manners at Mealtime

We have now covered the full range of dining etiquette, from appetizers to the main course, dessert, and your full conduct at the table. In this final chapter, I share a mix of reminders and new tips to help you navigate mealtime manners with confidence. Whether it's your first dinner party or your one hundredth, by following these guidelines, you'll remain poised and polished at the dining table.

1. Be mindful of your posture when eating. Sit up straight with your feet flat on the floor.

2. Keep in mind, nothing belongs on the table except for food.

3. Keep your phone off the table, use it only if it relates to the conversation with your fellow diners, and step away from the table to take a call.

4. Do not place your handbag on the table.

5. It is acceptable to have a small writing pad or notebook on the table when taking a business or planning meeting.

6. Place your napkin in your lap with the fold toward you and use a small corner to gently dab your mouth as needed.

7. If you should sneeze, cough, or burp, turn your head away from the table then sneeze, cough, or burp into your napkin.

8. When burping, don't open your mouth too wide. Keep your lips closer together so the sound is not loud.

9. Be sure to say, "Excuse me" after you have burped.

10. If you must blow your nose or leave the table for any reason, simply excuse yourself. However, there is no need to tell people what you are going to do. So don't say "I have to go blow my nose", or "I have to pick this thing out of my teeth."

11. If you must leave the table, slightly fold your napkin and place it to the LEFT of your place setting. Be sure to put the napkin back on your lap once you have returned to the table.

12. Use all eating utensils properly. Be sure to practice when at home.

13. Use utensils from the "outside in." That is the basic rule for navigating any formal place setting.

14. A way to recall how your personal place setting is arranged is to visualize BMW = Starting from your left you have your Bread, Meal, and Water in that order.

15. You can also use the number of letters that correspond with the utensils: "Fork" has the same number of letters in "Left." "Knife" has the same number of letters as "Right."

16. Another easy way to remember which side your bread and drink belong on is to use your hands. Form a circle with your thumb and index finger on each hand, extending the other fingers straight. When you look down at your hands, your left hand will form a 'b' for bread, and your right hand will form a 'd' for drink.

17. Avoid putting too much food on your fork. It makes it too easy to overstuff your mouth.

18. Take small bites and take your time to savor your food when you eat.

19. Don't reach for things at the table; ask to have them passed to you.

20. Always pass items around the table to the right.

21. Do not lick your fingers or any of your eating utensils.

22. Don't pick your teeth at the table, and don't hide behind a napkin. Excuse yourself from the table and take care of it in the restroom.

23. Do not lean backwards in your chair.

24. Always lift your glass or cup to your face. Do not hunch over the table and sip, even if you have a straw.

25. Keep your elbows off the table unless you're between courses or the table is clear of food.

26. Chew with your mouth closed. It is upsetting when people can see chewed-up food in your mouth.

27. Salt and pepper are always passed around the table together.

28. Do not reach over the table to shake hands. Instead, nod politely when you meet someone or greet someone.

29. You may converse with your tablemates that are on the left and the right of you.

30. When sitting at a large table, do not feel compelled to speak to the individuals on the other side of the table.

31. If you arrive at the table after others are seated, do not go around the table and shake hands with each individual. Simply greet everyone at once, then take your seat.

32. When you're being served your meal, you must wait until each individual is served at the table before you begin to eat.

33. If one person's food arrives later or the host's food arrives later and they instruct everyone to begin their meal, graciously oblige that individual and eat your meal.

34. If you're eating at a buffet-style meal in a public setting, for example, a wedding, you must wait until at least half of the individuals have returned to the table before you begin to eat.

    o   For example, if you're sitting at a table of eight, wait until at least four individuals have returned to the table.

    o   If you're sitting at a table with an odd number of people, for example, a table of five, then wait until at least three individuals have returned to the table before you begin to eat.

35. Always return to the buffet with a clean plate.

36. If you are in a private home and only one plate is distributed for each individual, you would use your one plate when returning to the buffet. Try to scrape it clean before you return.

37. When at a restaurant and the wait staff comes to remove your plates and cutlery from the table, do not dodge back and forth from side to side. Instead, remain still and allow them to reach on your left or right side to collect the items.

38. Once you begin the meal, your utensils should not be placed back on the table.

39. Whenever a course is complete, whether they were used or not, be sure to place any utensils meant for that particular course onto the plate.

40. Do not push your plates or cutlery away from you when you're finished eating; simply allow the waitstaff to collect it for you.

41. Do not stack plates on top of one another when you are done eating at a restaurant. Lifting heavy stacks of plates can be a challenge. Most servers have a planned way of balancing the plates. Furthermore, if food is stuck to the bottom of the plate, it can be uncomfortable for the server.

42. When you are finished with your meal, slightly fold your napkin and place it to the LEFT of your place setting.

43. Push your chair in when you leave the table.

44. If you are at home, help to clear your utensils from the table.

CHAPTER 16

Table Settings and Service: A Visual Guide

BASIC TABLE SETTING

Use this section as a visual reference to reinforce everything you've learned so far. My goal is for you to feel confident and at ease, whether you're dining out, networking, or hosting at home. Set the table a few times each week, and consider adding linen napkins for a beautiful, reusable touch that elevates the experience.

Basic Table Setting   *Soup Only Table Setting*   *Tea Table Setting*

FORMAL TABLE SETTING

This formal place setting is typically used for elegant dinners and multi-course meals. While you may not use it at home, understanding each element helps you feel poised and prepared in upscale dining situations.

A	Butter Knife	F	White Wine Glass	K	Entree Knife
B	Bread Plate	G	Red Wine Glass	L	Charger
C	Desert Fork	H	Champagne Glass	M	Dinner Knife
D	Desert or Teaspoon	I	Napkin	N	Salad Knife
E	Water Goblet	J	Salad Fork	O	Soup Spoon

HOW TO REMEMBER YOUR TABLE SETTING

Earlier in the book, I shared a few simple tricks to help you remember which parts of the place setting are yours. These diagrams serve as a visual reminder to reinforce those tips.

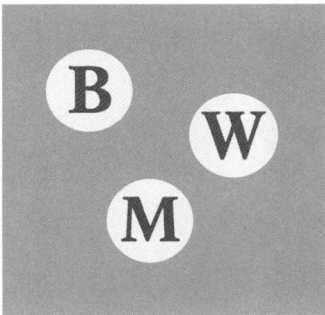

Bread - Meal - Water   *Bread and Drinks*   *Same Number of Letters*

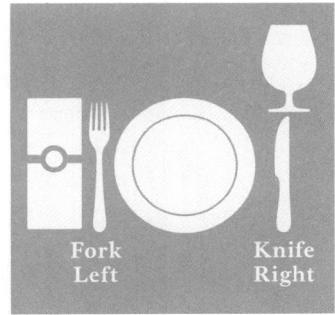

HOW TO HOLD YOUR UTENSILS

Holding Your Fork and Kinfe

Hold your fork in your left hand, with the handle resting in the palm of your hand and your index finger placed along the back of the fork. Hold your knife in your right hand in the same manner. The handle in your palm and your index finger along the back of the knife. If you are left-handed or feel that one hand is more dominant, you may switch hands. The key is to ensure you are holding your utensils properly, using your fingers rather than gripping them with your fist.

Holding Your Fork   *Holding Your Spoon*

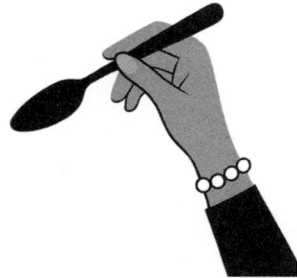

DINING SIGNALS

This is how to place your utensils at different points during your meal.

Resting Position: American Style   *Resting Position: Continental Style*

Finished Position: American and Continental Style

Although the dining styles differ, the finished position for both American and Continental styles is the same: the fork and knife are placed side by side at the 4 o'clock position on the plate. The only difference is in the fork's placement. The tines face upward for American style and downward for Continental style.

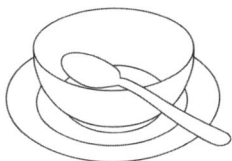

Soup Spoon: Resting Position

Soup Spoon: Finished Position

HOW TO HOLD CUPS AND GLASSES

These illustrations demonstrate the proper way to hold various glasses and cups. Each image reflects the guidance provided earlier in the book. Use these visuals as a guide to help you practice proper dining etiquette in everyday situations.

Holding a Tea Cup

Holding a Coffee Mug

Holding a Water Goblet

*Holding a Red
or White Wine Glass*

*Holding a
Champagne Glass*

HOW TO POUR WINE AND CHAMPAGNE

Pour wine just below the widest part of the glass to allow for proper aeration. For champagne, fill no more than two-thirds full to preserve the bubbles and prevent overflow.

Pour wine just below the widest part of the glass.

For champagne, fill no more than two-thirds full to preserve the bubbles and prevent overflow.

UTENSILS

Dessert Fork · Entree Fork · Oyster Fork · Salad & Appetizer Fork · Butter Knife · Entree Knife · Fish Knife · Salad & Appetizer Knife · Steak Knife

Demitasse Spoon · Dessert Spoon · Grapefruit Spoon · Iced Tea Spoon · Soup Spoon · Escargot Tongs · Shellfish Cracker · Shellfish Pick

GLASSWARE

Beer Mug · Brandy Snifter · Champagne Glass · Coupe · Dessert Wineglass · Highball Glass · Pint Glass

Martini Glass · Red Wine Glass · Rocks Glass · Sherry Glass · Shot Glass · Water Goblet · White Wine Glass

PART FOUR

Professional Etiquette and Business *Success*

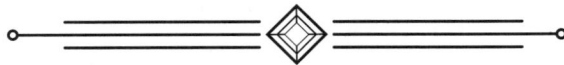

BUILDING A POLISHED PRESENCE IN THE
WORKPLACE AND BEYOND

In professional spaces, the most powerful form of communication is how you make others feel respected.

- ELAINE SWANN -

CHAPTER 17:

Professional Presence and Networking

In professional spaces, the most powerful form of communication is how you make others feel respected. Your success in the workplace isn't just measured by your skill—it is shaped by your personal presence, your professionalism, and the ability to communicate effectively. These chapters are your guide to thriving in the business environment, from the job interview to the boardroom, to the business meeting over a meal, to the social business event and beyond. You'll learn how to make introductions, manage a variety of workplace dynamics, navigate networking events, and lead with authenticity. Because the most polished professionals aren't just efficient at their job, they're also empathetic and aware of how they show up in the work environment. It's your etiquette in this instance that will set you apart and elevate your professional presence.

BUSINESS INTRODUCTIONS

The foundational etiquette for introducing yourself and others—such as standing, smiling, offering a firm handshake, and stating your first and last name—is outlined in the "Introductions" section at the beginning of this book. In professional settings, these guidelines still apply, with a few important additions:

Include your title when appropriate. While it's generally best to leave titles out in social settings, in business, your role (e.g., CEO, director of operations, lead consultant) can provide clarity and credibility.

Always introduce clients first. Clients and customers take precedence in introductions, no matter their age or title. For example:

"Mr. Client, I'd like you to meet our director of marketing, Clinton Gorham."

Clarify professional relationships. Use terms like "colleague," "project manager," or "vendor partner" to give context and make others feel at ease.

When making group introductions, such as to a team or department, a general introduction is fine (e.g., "William, I'd like you to meet the members of our leadership team."), followed by individual names and roles as appropriate.

If you're the highest-ranking person in the room, take the lead in making introductions to model professionalism for others.

While the mechanics of introductions remain the same, these business nuances help elevate your presence and leave a lasting impression.

CHIVALRY IN THE WORKPLACE

In the workplace, chivalry is gender-free and mutual. No matter male or female, always extend courtesies to your coworkers.

SHAKING HANDS	*A man does not need to wait for a woman to offer her hand today, especially in business. Whether you're a man or woman, just go ahead and shake hands.*
HOLDING DOORS.	*Whoever gets to the door first should hold it for others.*
PAYING FOR A BUSINESS MEAL	*Whoever does the inviting should pay.*
GETTING ON AND OFF ELEVATORS	*The person that is closest to the elevator door exits first.*
HELPING TO CARRY SOMETHING	*If anyone is overloaded with books, packages, or cumbersome items, whoever is nearby should always offer to help.*
HELPING TO PUT ON A COAT	*If someone is having difficulty putting on their coat or sweater, help should be offered.*
STANDING	*Regardless of gender, standing is a polite way of greeting someone, especially when a person is of higher rank or authority, a client, or elderly.*

NETWORKING ETIQUETTE GUIDELINES

Dress appropriately. Wear clothes that fit well and are appropriate for the event. This is not the time to show off to the guys or ladies that you have a fabulous body. Choose comfortable yet stylish attire. It's hard to mingle with confidence if your clothes are ill-fitting or if you're dressed inappropriately.

Check your cell phone at the door. Don't even think of chatting on your cell phone during a function. If you are expecting an important call that can't be dealt with by voicemail, then excuse yourself at the time you are expecting the call and step outside away from the crowd. Keep your call brief.

When greeting people in any business or personal situation, if you have to wonder if a hug is appropriate, then it probably is not.

Create an engaging self-introduction. Practice your introduction on every occasion. It shouldn't sound like a sales pitch; just keep it simple, pleasant, and sincere.

Bring plenty of business cards. Running out of business cards will prevent you from leaving people with a means to contact you. If a person has your business card on hand, they'll also be able to remember who you are and what you do. Don't rely on little pieces of paper or napkins that can get lost.

Keep your business cards under control. Don't just thrust your business card at a person as a self-introduction. Let people see the human side of you and engage in good conversation first. Then, if the opportunity lends itself, ask for their business card and then offer yours.

The proper way to hand your business card over to an individual is to pass it to them right side up. The recipient should be able to look down directly at the details on your card without having to turn it around. Present your business card in the same professional manner you would present yourself.

If you see people exchanging cards, don't just stick your hand in the mix and ask for their card like it's a flier. Business cards are an exchange of personal information; therefore, you should make a personal connection with them before requesting a card.

If you have a digital business card on your phone, be sure to move the app to the homepage of your screen. This way, you can open your phone and access it easily. You don't want to keep a person waiting while you fumble through multiple pages on your phone.

Be prepared to introduce yourself to new people. Your purpose for attending the event should be to meet new people and build new relationships. You can't do so if you clam up and keep to yourself or clump together with only people you know. Try to introduce yourself to at least three new people you do not know.

When you arrive at a networking event, one thing you most often receive is a name tag. The proper placement for your name tag is on the right-hand side just below your shoulder blade. We place it here so that when you move your right hand forward to shake hands, your shoulder will go in that direction and move slightly forward, then people will clearly be able to see your name.

Steer clear of political, religious, or lifestyle debates. These topics can quickly lead to tension or arguments, especially when alcohol is involved. Unless you are among like-minded company, it is best to keep those opinions to yourself.

Have something to talk about. Stay informed on current events by reading the news, newspapers, and industry magazines. A little celebrity gossip can help too. People often mention pop culture while making a point, and you do not want to be left nodding without a clue.

Approach conversations with ease. Many people appear tense at business events, with tight posture, stiff smiles, or avoiding eye contact. Instead, greet others with warmth. Relax your shoulders, stand tall, and make eye contact. Confidence is often just perception.

Get comfortable starting conversations. Look for everyday chances to connect, like greeting someone at a coffee shop or chatting with a store clerk. Use these moments to build your confidence so professional networking feels more natural.

Follow the 10-5 rule. If you make eye contact with someone within ten feet of you, you should acknowledge them with a nod or a smile. At five feet, you should say something, "Hello," or "Good evening." It's a good rule because it sometimes drives people crazy when others pretend they don't see them!

Have a positive attitude. Remember the three Es: Energy, Effort, and Enthusiasm. Look like you want to be there, like you're having fun. Be positive, be friendly, and make everyone feel special.

Be considerate. Sometimes it's easy to forget to use kind words such as "Please," "Thank you," "Yes, please," and "No, thank you." Be sure to do so.

While I covered some of this in the dining section, it's worth repeating here because these moments often happen during business networking events too.

Don't reach over a dining table to shake hands. Just greet the person with a slight nod and a polite smile.

Mind your table manners. Use the correct eating utensils. No double dipping, no burping, and picking, talking with food in your mouth, nothing unbecoming or unsightly.

Keep your drink in your left hand. Leave your right hand available to shake hands without a wet handshake from your drink.

If you are holding an appetizer plate, hold it in your right hand, and use your left hand to eat your finger foods. Then you go to greet someone, switch the plate to your left hand, and shake hands with that right hand. You can always switch back once you have completed the greeting. This way, you can avoid transferring germs to your food or shake the person's hand with greasy fingers.

Exit lines help you leave a conversation without feeling awkward. Saying goodbye is just as important as saying hello. Keep it simple and genuine. Try something like, "It was great chatting," or "I'll let you mingle, but I hope we cross paths again soon."

Remember, it's still a business gathering. Even though you may feel inclined to do so, this is not the time to let your hair down and get too relaxed. In fact, keep your hair up (figuratively speaking). Watch what you say, whom you say it to, and how you behave. Your behavior tonight will still impact how much you're respected, whether you build a great connection, and how you're perceived the next day at work.

Don't drink too much. Regardless of your tolerance level, make it a two-drink-maximum night. No if, ands, or buts about this one. You want to always maintain self-control, and the best way to do it is to drink very little or not at all.

When attending business functions, you may be offered an alcoholic beverage. If you prefer not to drink, whether in general or just for the evening, simply decline with grace and without explanation. A polite "No, thank you" is enough. You can also request an alternative, like sparkling water with lime or cranberry juice. Avoid sharing personal stories or reasons for not drinking, as these moments are not the time for deep disclosures. Keep the focus on the event, not your beverage choices.

Gracefully enter a group conversation. When we arrive at events, your desire should be to connect with key people who are present. Sometimes they might appear preoccupied if they are gathered in a small group. It is acceptable to approach that group and gain entry into their conversation. Here's how to best go about it.

- Approach the group and share a pleasant smile when doing so.

- Try to make eye contact with at least one individual, especially if there's someone in the group that you know.

- If you don't know anyone there, then get close to the group and nod at someone as you join in.

- Engage in the conversation and listen to what's being said. Interact with them. When they laugh, you laugh, but don't overdo it and call too much attention to yourself.

- The moment someone opens up and shows you a bit of welcoming open body language, this is a moment that you can briefly introduce yourself.

- Briefly say your name, shake hands if time allows, and then continue engaging in the conversation.

- You can even get the conversation going again by interjecting a question or a clever statement about what has already been said.

Know when to make your exit. Know when to leave a person, a group, or a function. Use something like, "It's been great talking with you; enjoy the rest of your evening."

Thank your host or committee members. If you can thank them that night, then do so. If not, then send an email if you received an email invitation or a note if you received a written invitation. They've worked hard to make sure your office has an opportunity to network and socialize, so be kind and simply say thank you.

CONVEYING POLITENESS, RESPECT, AND KINDNESS AT THE OFFICE PARTY

When it comes to office parties, I always say to treat it like another level of a job interview or career advancement. You are being watched. Your social skills, your ability to connect, and how well you fit in with the team all matter. This is your opportunity for people to see that you are likable and approachable, so do not skip it. Even if you only attend for a short while, your presence shows that you are a team player, and yes, it is noticed who does not show up. Ask someone about a vacation they took, or if you are going to talk about work, compliment a colleague on an achievement or milestone. As the evening unfolds, stay grounded and gracious. Let your presence leave a lasting impression. "This is someone I'd like to work with."

HOW TO DECLINE AFTER-WORK HANGOUT INVITES FROM COWORKERS

When it comes to declining an after-work hangout with a coworker who might be adamant about spending time with you, just look at the three core values: respect, honesty, and consideration. Just be honest with the person. It's going to be a little bit icky, and it might feel hard because you don't want to hurt their feelings. This might be an awkward moment, but the important thing is that you just tell your absolute truth.

Just say to the person, "I make it a practice not to hang out with coworkers after work. It's just a personal choice I have. But if you want to get together for coffee during the workday or go out to lunch, then let's do that." Give them some sort of alternative.

Now, don't go into detail about any past experiences because then the individual might take it personally or might think that you're talking about them. In the end, you may feel a little bit awkward about it, but you will be known as the person who doesn't hang out with coworkers after work. And honestly, that is a pretty good place to be—if it's something that you truly don't want to do.

CHAPTER 18

Workplace Behavior and Communication

WHEN A COWORKER ANSWERS YOUR QUESTION BEFORE YOU FINISH ASKING

When you're talking with someone and asking a question, and they interrupt you with their answer, do this:

1. Pause.

2. Let them finish.

3. Give it a beat.

4. Smile.

5. Then ask your question again.

This teaches them to wait until you are finished speaking before they respond.

HOW TO HANDLE A COLLEAGUE WHEN THEY INTERRUPT YOU

You're at work, having a one-on-one conversation with a colleague, and they interrupt you. Grab back your power in that conversation and hold your space by doing two things. First, use both your words and your body language. Hold one hand up in a gentle 'stop' gesture as you speak to help reinforce your message. Say, "Hold on, I'm going to interrupt you right there. I know you probably have something you'd like to share, but I would like to finish my thought first." Then continue with, "So, anyway, as I was saying, what I think we should do is . . ." and just keep your conversation going. Don't let people take over the conversation. It is absolutely acceptable for you to interrupt someone and hold your space.

HOW TO PROPERLY ADDRESS SNARKY REMARKS DURING AN IN-PERSON MEETING

You're in a meeting, and someone at the table says something snarky or disrespectful to you. Here's how you handle it. Pause. Don't say anything at all. Allow that person to make eye contact with you. Once they do, say, "Is there something you wanted to share?" Say it calmly, without a nasty tone or negative body language. Be genuinely interested. Most of the time, the person will say, "Oh, no, nothing at all." Or they might say, "Yes, I do have something." That's when you keep your power and respond, "Alright, thank you. Why don't we wait until after we're done, and then you can address it." This is how you put the person in their place, take your power back in a very polite manner, and keep the meeting going.

HOW TO PROPERLY HANDLE SNARKY COMMENTS IN A VIRTUAL MEETING

You're in a virtual meeting, and someone makes a snarky comment, but you can't quite tell who it is in that sea of squares. Do not let that person have the floor. Don't let them take over your meeting. Instead, say, "I'm not sure who made the comment, but I'd love to talk with you after the meeting. Just send me a private message in the chat, and I'll be sure to follow up with you." Then go right back to your agenda: "So, anyway, folks, as I was saying . . ." and keep your meeting going. Don't give that person the floor. Don't give them the power to take over your conversation or derail what you're saying in the meeting.

HOW TO PROPERLY HANDLE WHEN YOUR BOSS MAKES A SNARKY REMARK

You're hosting a meeting, you're speaking, and you hear your boss make a snarky comment. What do you do in that moment? Here's what you don't do. Don't stop the meeting to address it. Just keep talking, act as if you never heard it, and finish the meeting. Afterwards, I do want you to approach that person with respect and dignity. Say, "I thought I heard you say something during the meeting, and I'm not quite sure if you were trying to get my attention to address something. Did you want to give some feedback? I'm open to hearing whatever you have to share." Then stop and allow them to speak. Nine times out of ten, they might say it was nothing, because maybe they were just being rude. But if they had something valid to say, sit, listen, take it in, and have that dialogue. The important thing is to get clarity and make sure it wasn't something real that needed to be addressed.

Tread lightly when it comes to that authority figure in the workplace, so be mindful of your tone and your body language during this exchange.

PROFANITY AND PROFESSIONALISM

Many individuals use profanity to emphasize their point or a specific emotion. The key to keep in mind is that profanity might be offensive to others. It can damage your credibility, and people might deal with you differently if they don't care for the language. In tense situations, profanity might escalate emotions and cause an argument or misunderstanding.

HANDLING SENSITIVE CONVERSATIONS IN THE WORKPLACE

Workplace relationships are professional, but we still experience real-life events side by side with our coworkers. It's important to show care and compassion when sensitive topics come up.

In Chapter 6, Thank-You Notes, Gifts, and Thoughtful Responses, we covered what to say and what not to say during personal milestones like illness, loss, marriage, and more. The same principles apply in the workplace: Think twice before you speak, listen more than you talk, and offer support without being pushy.

Remember that in professional settings, a little discretion goes a long way. It's often best to keep your comments brief, kind, and appropriate to the nature of your relationship. Sometimes a simple "I'm so sorry to hear that" or "Congratulations to you and your family" is all that's needed.

SETTING BOUNDARIES PROFESSIONALLY

- For the person who offers you advice when it's none of their business.
  - o Say, "Thanks for your input. I'll keep that in mind."

- Somebody comes to you with their work problem, and they want you to help fix it.
  - o Don't take on other people's problems. Instead, say, "I understand that falls into the scope of your responsibility, but I'm happy to help wherever it's feasible for me."

- You are asked to stay late at work.
  - o Do not do it. Don't make a habit of it. Just tell the individual this: "My workday ends at five, but I'll prioritize this first thing tomorrow or Monday."

WORKSPACE MANAGEMENT

CUBICLES

- Don't just barge into someone's space. Knock lightly or say, "May I come in?"
- No "prairie dogging." Don't stand or pop up constantly to talk to coworkers in the area or hang over someone else's cubicle. If someone does this to you repeatedly, politely ask them to come around to speak with you instead.
- Speak softly when talking on the phone or to coworkers who are visiting your space.
- Never shout information or requests back and forth throughout the office.

- Keep music low or use headphones if your company allows it.

- If your neighbors are loud, be polite when asking them to quiet down.

- If you have a visitor or a brief meeting, move to a common work area.

OFFICE WITH A DOOR

Close the door only when necessary, such as for visitors or confidential meetings. Do not close the door to make personal calls all day long or to perform personal tasks. Never slam the door; it could be misconstrued as aggressive or offensive. If people outside the office are talking loudly, close the door softly.

WORKSPACE DECOR

Be mindful of the type of jokes, cartoons, or sayings posted around the workspace so that it does not offend your coworkers. Do not post any company- or competitor-bashing signs or materials. Know and follow company standards.

WORKSPACE MANNERS

- Burping, slurping, loud yawning, and relieving yourself of bodily discomfort are out.

- A quick nose blow at your desk is acceptable, but if it becomes prolonged, you should head to the bathroom.

- Stand for the superior, elderly, your clients, and prospective clients. This is not necessarily etiquette, but it shows a sign of respect. This includes coworkers who you may not have seen in a while or ones that you don't see regularly.

- Eat quietly and use good manners. Also, if you bring your own lunch, be mindful of the smell that certain foods may have.

- Always take meetings in an appropriate location. Don't invade another's workspace, even if you are a supervisor.

- If a visitor comes to the office, always have them wait in the reception area and then notify the person they are there to see. Never let a person walk through the office.

- If you have visitors, be sure to walk them back out to the reception area.

- When you're passing by your coworkers, be sure to greet one another at the beginning of each day. Afterward, a smile, nod, or brief "How's it going?" is sufficient.

COMMUNITY WORKSPACE MANNERS

PRINTER

- If you have a big copy job, allow someone with a smaller job to go first.

- After a big print job, double-check the paper supply and refill it if necessary.

- Be sure to abide by company policy when it comes to using the copier.

- If you see someone's document in the machine, don't just throw it to the side. Instead, leave it face up so that they can see it, or place it in the designated space.

- If the machine breaks down or needs servicing, be kind to the support technician who is there to service it.

FURNITURE

Treat the office furniture with the same care and respect you would show if you were a guest in someone else's home. Handle chairs, desks, and other items gently, and avoid causing unnecessary wear or damage.

KITCHEN

Clean up after yourself after preparing and eating food. Remove your food from the refrigerator in a timely manner and clean up any spills or soakings. If something boils over in the microwave, clean it up immediately. Do not leave dirty mugs or dishes in the sink; wash your dishes as soon as you finish your meal.

RESTROOMS

- Wipe up any splashed water from around the sink after you've used it to keep the area clean, dry, and presentable for the next person.

- When it comes to makeup, shaving, or brushing your teeth, remember you are not at home, so be mindful of taking over the space.

- If an air freshener is supplied, be sure to use it after yourself, especially if you leave behind strong odors. Using the air freshener helps keep the shared space clean, fresh, and pleasant for everyone.

CHAPTER 19

Business Meetings and Conferences

MEETING ETIQUETTE DO'S AND DON'TS

DON'T NOT SHOW UP

It's always tempting to remain at your desk and keep working, but rather than sending a signal of being a hard worker, you'll just end up offending the party who called the meeting. It's important to understand that meetings also foster an environment to build relationships, which is vital to your success.

DON'T SHOW UP LATE

Nothing says "I don't have my stuff together" like walking into a meeting that's already in progress. Arriving a few minutes early not only demonstrates that you respect your colleagues' time, but it also guarantees you get a good seat.

DON'T ARRIVE UNPREPARED

Be sure you have any materials or reports prepared and on hand prior to your arrival. If pertinent information or memos have been distributed beforehand, read them and familiarize yourself with the subject matter. In addition, if you have any questions, comments, or contributions, have them written down so you can refer to them during the meeting.

DON'T LEAVE YOUR CELL PHONE ON

Keep your phone on silent. Forget the vibrate function as well, because merely looking at your phone can be a distraction to the meeting presenter and those around you. Oh, and NEVER, NEVER take a call in the middle of a meeting.

DON'T DOMINATE THE CONVERSATION

Once the actual discussion has begun, allow the more senior figures to make their contribution first. It's alright to interject and make your point, but keep it simple, and stay on track. Plus, you don't have to comment on every issue at hand. Take time out to listen because you might just learn something.

DON'T MAKE YOUR STATEMENTS SOUND LIKE QUESTIONS

Once you frame your thought as a question, you invite others to respond and potentially take credit for solving your "question." Instead, make it a firm, declarative statement.

DON'T DEVIATE FROM THE TOPIC

Don't go off on a tangent and start bringing up things that have nothing to do with the discussion at hand. Having notes or making notes during the discussion will assist you with staying on task. If you think of something that may relate to another topic, write that down and then be prepared to address it at the next appropriate meeting.

DON'T ALLOW YOURSELF TO BE INTIMIDATED

Some folks will look at meetings as an opportunity to bash other coworkers in order to make themselves look better. Don't fall into this trap and lay down like a wounded puppy, nor should you come back swinging and make a mess of things. If you are attacked, just stand your ground, politely defend yourself, and, if necessary, be politely frank when putting the attacker back on track.

RULES FOR POST-CONFERENCE CONDUCT

The meeting has concluded, and guests are beginning to mingle. Your presentation earned the respect of many, as you were both knowledgeable and comical about the issue at hand. The last thing that you want to do now is lose the admiration of colleagues with poor conduct. Here, then, are four rules to follow while conversing with business professionals after a meeting.

RULE #1: DON'T DRINK TOO MUCH

Remember that this is a business setting, and the rules about drinking still apply. Socializing while indulging in a glass of wine is okay. Taking the whole bottle as your own is not good.

RULE #2: TAKE FULL ADVANTAGE OF THE OPPORTUNITY TO GET TO KNOW COLLEAGUES

Now is your time to learn what your coworkers do when away from the job. Gain knowledge of what their hobbies are and how they spend weekends with the family by listening and asking questions along the way. Make sure that your questions are not too intrusive and rely on their body language to tell you if an inquiry is too personal.

RULE #3: HAVE INTERESTING TOPICS TO DISCUSS

Perhaps you are shy or maybe your personality is insolent to the point of others being turned off. You should consider doing additional research to find topics to discuss during the meet-and-greet segment. Current events, except for politics and religion, are always a good place to search as they are great conversation starters.

RULE #4: SET UP A TIME TO MEET WITH COLLEAGUES AFTER WORK, AND CHOOSE AN ACTIVITY THAT EVERYONE WILL ENJOY

If you propose the idea of meeting outside of the general gathering, think inside of the box. Consider what colleagues have said about their hobbies and select an outing that agrees with the majority.

Keep in mind that the activity is with colleagues, so going out to the club may not be the best idea, even if the majority agrees. Remember to be creative yet sensible when choosing activities for your day out.

BUSINESS TRIP

You're going on your first business trip and are overcome with excitement. After several years with the company, you are finally being trusted to represent the brand outside of an ordinary day on the job. This opportunity could establish you as a driving force in the corporation or lead to you being crowned the weakest leak. Much of your success, or failure, depends on preparation and etiquette.

WHEN YOU RUN INTO YOUR BOSS OUTSIDE OF WORK: 4 TIPS

Spotting your boss outside of the workplace can be both pleasurable and stressful. How should you approach your superior, and what should you say to them? Here are a few tips.

TIP #1: LEAVE WORK TALK OUT OF IT

This is not the time to complain about the job or go into great detail about what you think needs to be done differently or better. Don't take it upon yourself to lay into them about whatever is going on at the office.

TIP #2: DON'T OVERSTAY YOUR WELCOME

It's alright for you to acknowledge them when you see them. It is important, however, to be brief and polite. Simply say, "Hello," share some niceties, and keep it moving. Remember that your boss is your boss, and it may be a bit awkward to see them outside of work. Even if you are best friends at work, you're not necessarily best friends when you are out and about. Also, remember not to invade your boss's space. Just because you know them, it doesn't mean that you should join them during their time of dining out at a restaurant or walk alongside them as they shop. Also, pay attention to body language. Certain gestures will tell you if they are open and accepting of your approach or if you are overstaying your welcome.

TIP #3: DON'T TAKE BACK WHAT YOU SEE TO THE OFFICE

If you saw the boss out with her family or friend, just keep it to yourself. Refrain from making such sighting office news the next day. You never know if what you saw was something you were supposed to see, and you certainly don't want to be the one to bring back any information that probably should not be shared. Remember that you saw them at a private time in their life and, as such, it's polite to help them maintain such privacy.

TIP #4: DON'T TALK ABOUT BUSINESS

Refrain from bringing up topics that warrant a scheduled meeting at work. This includes asking about a raise or seeking advice on a project. These conversations are best reserved for the office, where they can be handled professionally.

CHAPTER 20

Business Dining Etiquette

THE ART OF THE BUSINESS MEAL

- Who - You and your client, potential client, or business associate.
  - o This is when your conversational abilities, self-control, and table manners are all on display at once. This all reflects on you and the company you represent, the job you want to get, or the client you want to land.

- What - A meeting with food.
  - o The meeting can take place at a restaurant, club, private home, and office. It can range from casual to formal.

- When - Breakfast, lunch, or dinner.
  - o Breakfast - Many people are sharper in the morning because they're not bogged down with the day's business. It can be a short and focused occasion. Less costly.

- Lunch – Doesn't cut into personal time. It can last just over an hour to two hours. Stays relatively short and focused because it's in the middle of the workday.

- Dinner – Can be for two or a large group. It may last longer and is more leisurely. Generally geared towards camaraderie. It can be an advantage when doing serious business is the goal.

- Where – Location, location, location!
  - It depends on which meal you'll have – breakfast, lunch, or dinner.
  - Pick a place you've eaten at before.
  - If you are the host, consider your guest's preference, allergies, etc.
  - Choose a location that is easy to find with ample parking.
  - Consider the noise factor. If you want to talk, a loud place may not be the best fit.

- Why – It's a covert operation!
  - To gather information and learn more about your business associate that can be helpful to your relationship.
  - To create an opportunity for quality time and a more personal connection with business associates.
  - To take your business relationship to a higher level.

BEFORE YOU GO

- Determine who the host is. The best way to find out is to just ask! You can say:

    o   "Will you be my guest?"

    o   "I'd like to invite you . . ."

    o   "Would you like to split lunch?" (For someone you dine with more frequently.)

- Make reservations, if possible.

- Do your homework. Prepare business information to share, and do research on your lunch mate, their company, and the industry. Explore current events for small talk.

- If you're the host, have a backup plan. Anything can happen, so it's good to be prepared to make changes.

- Dress appropriately by wearing polished, professional attire that matches the tone of the meeting and shows respect for the occasion.

- Arrive on time. Wait for your host if they haven't arrived yet. They may have a specific table, server, or section of the restaurant they prefer. So, it's best for you to wait for them to arrive instead of being seated.

NAVIGATING THE BUSINESS MEAL

- Control your cell phone. The cell phone should only be used when it has something to do with the conversation at hand. Otherwise, it should remain in your pocket or your bag, not on top of the dining table.

- "Please" and "Thank you" still go a long way. Mind your manners by being polite to the wait staff and practice good table manners. Place your napkin in your lap. Know the silverware and stemware placement, etc.

- To drink or not? Let your host set the tone, but it's alright to pass.

- Engage in thoughtful small talk. Ask questions rather than making statements. Ask about their interests, industry, business, and future plans. Remember to listen and respond to what's being said. Note: It's a conversation, not an interrogation.

- Don't overindulge with your meal choice. It's best to order medium-priced dishes. A good way to gauge what to order is to ask the host, "What would you suggest?" or "What are you going to have?"

- Choose something that is easy to eat. Stay away from stringy foods such as spaghetti and linguine. Oversized burgers and sandwiches can be a bit messy. Never go with really messy foods such as crab or lobster unless you are invited to a restaurant for that specific type of meal.

- The business discussion will most likely take place after the meal is ordered. During dinner, it's usually after the main course is finished.

WRAP IT UP

- Once the meal or business is nearly finished, begin to wrap it up. This is a good time to really pay attention to body language.

- Bring the meal to a close by arranging your next meeting or confirming your next move.

- If you are the host, politely instruct the server to give you the bill and always pay with a credit card. If you are the attendee and not the host, refrain from offering to pay for a portion of the bill or the tip. It might offend your host.

- No doggie bags. Your time together is more about the business at hand and not necessarily the actual meal. Unless your host insists on you taking something home, there are no doggie bags for the business meal.

- Follow up. Say "Thank you" via card, note, or email. Follow through on any promises you may have made during the meal.

BUSINESS DINING: DO THIS, NEVER DO THAT

The art of dining out for business is often a slippery slope that many people descend with a quickness. While the majority of us know how to conduct ourselves during casual breakfast and dinner dates, eating while discussing business ventures is a different vein. We never quite know how much personality to give, and time is always a factor. Here are a few dos and don'ts of the business dining experience to abide by the next time you are invited to, or choose to host, one of these meetings.

Breakfast meetings should last a maximum of one hour, and midday luncheons have a two-hour cap. Arriving even ten minutes late at one of these gatherings means less discussion about the matter at hand. It is always better to be early than late when you are invited to meet and greet. You should definitely meet your party at the venue if you are hosting.

Do not keep guests at a dinner meeting for more than three hours. Patience runs thin, even with food on the table. As a host, it is your responsibility to keep things moving along and refrain from driving your guests to boredom. Never let them throw hints about the time. Instead, always be one step ahead in consideration. In any dinner setting, three hours is the maximum time that a meeting should last.

Select a restaurant that is conducive to conversation. Eateries in which guests have to yell in order to be heard are not the best places for business meetings. It is best to select a venue that is in line with the industry. If, for instance, you are meeting with marketing executives, you may want to select a spot that is more on the formal side of things. On the other hand, those who work in the entertainment industry may select a venue that is more liberal since the field is unconventional.

Do not offer to pay for the meal when invited, and do not accept payment when hosting. It is considered rude to offer payment, even a tip, when someone invites you to a business dinner. In the same vein, it is not proper to accept payment when hosting a meal engagement. Your invitation implies that all expenses are paid.

If you have a medical necessity, such as allergies or religious requirements, it's appropriate to mention it when asked. If you have a lifestyle choice, such as being vegan, keto, or other preferences, the polite thing to do is to navigate the menu quietly without making it the host's responsibility.

Do not ask for over-the-top substitutions. The purpose of business dining is to socialize. Your concern, as a guest, is to build new relationships and not necessarily about the food. It is, therefore, not the best idea to ask for substitutions to the menu. Such acts may be considered rude by the host.

Focus on the purpose of the meeting. It is good to socialize so that the person can learn more about you and feel better about doing business together. But you must remember that the theme of the meeting is business. Maintaining a balance between business and personal behavior is key to having a successful corporate dining experience.

CHAPTER 21

Business Travel and International Etiquette

BUSINESS TRAVEL

You've just received news that you will have to head out of town for a business trip. Whether this is your first, fifteenth, or fiftieth business trip, it's important to realize you have been trusted to represent the brand outside of an ordinary day on the job. This opportunity could establish you as a driving force in the corporation or lead to you being dubbed the weakest link. Much of your success or failure depends on preparation and consideration, and this begins before you go.

BEFORE YOU GO

Be self-reliant when traveling for business. The more prepared you are, the less you'll rely on others. Check if your hotel has a business center with essentials like Wi-Fi, printers, or computers. Check to see if your hotel has free Wi-Fi in advance or if there is an additional daily charge.

It is important to know this so you can work it into your travel plans. If you're going to meet a client at the hotel, call in advance to arrange a meeting room or convenient space located nearby.

If your journey is a long one, plan to arrive in town the day before your meeting or presentation. When you're booking your flights and any additional ground transportation, be sure to plan for any unexpected delays.

Once all of your arrangements are made, be sure to leave information with someone in your home office so they are aware of your full itinerary. Additionally, be sure to send any clients or individuals you're meeting at your destination details about your travel arrangements. It's the sort of thing that shows great consideration for all parties involved.

WHAT TO PACK

It's not a mere matter of packing but, rather, the way that you pack. Since there is always the possibility of your luggage getting lost when flying, you should store all important documents in your carry-on. You should also have at least two days' worth of business outfits packed in the carry-on to be completely prepared to move forward upon arriving at your destination. You can mix and match a few clothing pieces to make a complete outfit.

If you are giving a presentation, it's important to make sure you arrive fully prepared with any visual aids, such as a portfolio or PowerPoint presentation. It's a good idea to always back up your vital presentations digitally in some sort of online storage cloud as well.

Although travel arrangements are made electronically these days, I suggest you carry hard copies in your carry-on. Place them in a slim folder with everything printed out so you can take a glance at it if you don't have internet access or Wi-Fi or if your phone battery dies. Include your flight itinerary, hotel reservations, car reservations, and meeting places. If you're going to be driving, print out a map with driving directions in advance as well.

HOW TO DRESS

When traveling to another state or country, never assume anything. Whereas your definition of business attire may be on the side of semi-formal, the company that you visit may view jeans and a T-shirt as most appropriate. It is important to conduct research about the business and its culture before traveling. Remember that you want to stand out for all the right reasons. Failing to dress the part is not a good reason to gain attention.

UPON ARRIVAL

Connection is essential. Some travelers spend hours in the airport trying to find their business partners because they failed to develop a system by which they can find one another when the plane touches down. You should have a person of contact who you can inform when you have arrived. Such a person can also serve as a sort of tour guide who shows you the basics of the company and culture you are visiting.

BUSINESS TRAVELER MANNERS

When you arrive, whether your journey is via plane or train, be prepared to move swiftly through any security or check-in areas.

Don't set up a mini-office in the waiting room when you're traveling. Be mindful of others around you. Avoid spreading out everything from your laptop to reports and electronic devices.

It's important to recognize there are certain times during the year when a good deal of non-business travelers will be more present. Practice patience with these individuals, who would include families with small children, large groups of tourists, and the elderly.

When traveling by plane, keep in mind that the overhead bin does not have your name on it. It is shared with the rest of the travel community, so avoid commandeering the overhead bin with all your things.

Observe any posted guidelines or signs. An example would be the quiet car on a train where talking on your cell phone is not permitted.

If you have to take a telephone call, be sure you move out of the hearing range of others. Be mindful of your tone of voice if your conversation is prolonged. Most especially, refrain from divulging any sensitive company information, so be discreet in what you discuss.

If you're a frequent traveler, then you know what to expect with the travel process. Be patient with others; it's the polite thing to do.

TRAVELING WITH A COWORKER OR BOSS

Traveling with a coworker can be exciting. Spending time away from the routine of the office often affords the opportunity for personal growth and relationship expansion. Traveling with colleagues can be great, or a nightmare without proper manners.

REMEMBER THE TWO R'S

I suggest the two R's when traveling with a boss: one is **Respect,** the other one is **Reverence**. You don't have to overdo your behavior, but small courtesies such as allowing your boss to go ahead of you, making sure they have comfortable seating, and holding doors open are most appropriate. Use this opportunity to shine and let your boss see that you have the ability to take charge of various tasks. Minor acts such as making reservations, tipping any service individuals, checking in at your hotel, and double-checking on meeting rooms will place value on your ability to work with leadership.

ARRIVE ON TIME

The last thing that you want to do is hold up progress. Prepare for the flight, or drive, ahead of time and arrive at the agreed upon destination well in advance of takeoff. If you and a colleague are traveling by airplane, then you should make sure to be at least two hours early. This will give you ample time to go through security passage and close up other loose ends associated with departure.

LEAVE PERSONAL PROBLEMS AT HOME.

Your traveling partner came to conduct business. They should not serve as your second opinion on a family crisis. Do your best to keep personal conversations out of earshot so that your colleague is not subjected to the awkwardness that comes along with learning too much information about your personal life.

BE DISCREET

Keep private information private if you are on the receiving end of having knowledge of a colleague's personal struggles.

Let Anne Hathaway's character in The Devil Wears Prada be your guide. She did not disclose her boss' impending divorce even though such information was discovered during their business trip to Paris. Anne's character did everything within her power to shelter her boss, which is what you should do if you gain knowledge of privy information.

Don't just talk business while on the trip. Remember that this is a good time to connect with your colleague outside of the office. It's okay to engage in conversation that has little, if anything, to do with work.

DON'T BASH THE COMPANY

It's okay to agree that some changes in company policy might need to be made. It is not okay to present a laundry list of problems, such as criticizing the executive team for not taking a particular action. This is especially true when you are traveling with your boss.

DON'T ASK FOR A PAY INCREASE OR BONUS

You are building relationships, but not enough to ask for more money. If the subject is presented, let your boss lead discussions about compensation. Your focus should remain on being professional, reliable, and easy to travel with.

DON'T DISCONNECT

Make sure you stay connected to your party. There's nothing worse than traveling halfway across the country or even the world only to lose contact with your partner. If you plan on visiting friends or other colleagues while in town or going on an excursion or shopping trip or sightseeing, it's courteous to let the individual you're traveling with know where you are. Don't just assume they overheard you talking about your plans. Be clear and concise about your whereabouts and leave detailed information so you can be contacted at a moment's notice.

DINING COURTESY

If you're heading out to enjoy a great dining experience during your trip, be thoughtful and extend an invitation to your coworker. Even if they decline, giving them the option shows consideration. It would feel awful for them to find out later that you had a fantastic time at an exciting restaurant they might have wanted to try.

STAY CONNECTED

Staying connected means keeping your travel partner in the loop about your whereabouts. You don't have to invite them to every outing or excursion, but it's courteous to let them know if you plan to spend time off-site.

If you're meeting up with friends who are local to the area or taking some personal time, a simple heads-up helps to prevent any unnecessary worry or concern.

NAVIGATING BUSINESS IN DIFFERENT CULTURES

North American customs are much different from other parts of the world. Whereas handshakes are more common than hugs during business meetings in America, embracing before and after conferences is the norm in Central America. So how do you navigate the world of business with grace and eloquence when your way of life is greatly different from what you know? Here are a few tidbits to get you through the trip.

ON PERSONAL SPACE

In North America and Europe, individuals tend to stand two to three feet apart when conversing with one another. Japan and various parts of Asia stand even further apart. While North America and the United Kingdom keep their distance, the majority of the world conducts business in a more intimate manner. You should, therefore, not be surprised if you are warmly embraced by the CEO in a South American city. It's best to go with the flow of things and adjust your comfort levels.

BOWING

North Americans do not engage in much bowing during conferences. The same is not true in various parts of the world.

Japan, for instance, has a greeting system that calls for individuals with lower positions in the company to bob a little lower than those with more notable jobs. India does not utilize such a system, and individuals bow by placing their hands on their chest and nodding.

Since you may or may not be coming from a culture that is accustomed to bowing, it is best to wait for your host to either give a nod or handshake to partners. It is never a good idea to just assume that cultures within a region are alike. After all, China is in Asia and executives there prefer handshakes over bows.

ABOUT HANDSHAKES

North Americans tend to give firm handshakes. We believe that such action exudes confidence. In Asia soft handshakes are more common, and Germans have an accompanying bow or nod to go along with their hand greetings. Whereas everyone, men and women, shakes hands in France, it is considered highly offensive to offer a handshake to a woman in Islamic cultures.

The many variations in handshaking customs are all the more reason to do extensive research on the country that you are visiting. Searching the internet is a good way to start, and travel guides from the library are great for finalizing your investigation. When sifting through internet sites, be sure to check out blogs written by natives of the country.

MORE ON PREPARATION

It is essential to be mindful of religious holidays when doing business abroad. For example, Chinese cultures pause business during their New Year celebrations. You would, therefore, be unable to accomplish anything that involves a company or partner in the nation during this time. Having full knowledge of a country's calendar will save a lot of time and headache.

THE CUSTOM OF TIPPING

While tipping is a part of life in the United States, the act is not that popular in other regions of the world. Workers in Malaysia and Singapore do not expect a tip for services rendered, and it is considered an insult to give a little extra on the side in Japan. Imagine that!

When going the way of tips, first research the country you are visiting to make sure that it is permissible. You should also check rates so as not to give a worker too little for his service. Remember that tipping should be reserved for hotels, taxi rides and occasions of dining out. In no instance should you provide a tip when your host opts to pay for the meal.

COMMUNICATION

With the language barrier ever present during international interactions, it is important to remember that a translator is present to ensure that the conversation flows smoothly. They are not a part of the discussion in the sense of having knowledge about the matter at hand. You should, therefore, always keep your focus on the business partner you are engaging with, not the person providing interpretation. While it is rude to completely ignore the translator, your questions should never be directed towards them.

Another important thing to be mindful of is the fact that certain social media sites are not supported in every country. YouTube, for instance, is not a supported app in China. This means you may need to find alternative ways to share video content or presentations with clients, such as using local or approved platforms.

BUSINESS CARDS AND GIFTS

Unlike in the United States, where handing out business cards at social events is common, it is not always permissible to give out a contact card to prospective customers. In Italy, for instance, exchanging business cards outside of business meetings is not allowed. Although China is more flexible with business card exchange, presenting a card with both hands is still preferred. In general, check the local customs and always present your card right side up.

In addition to business cards, it is a good idea to bring gifts. You should not pay a lot for a present as partners may view it as a bribe. You should, however, purchase or make something that represents your brand and country.

THINGS TO AVOID

It is important to dress conservatively when meeting with fellow professionals. Men should wear suits that are tailored well while women should dress in a nice pants suit. Most countries prefer dresses over suits for women, but some nations take great pleasure in doing business with women who wear dresses.

While you should definitely dress to impress, it is equally important to converse with guests. Begin with the local news and work your way around the crowd if you are the shy type. In all cases, learn how to read body language so you will know when to pursue a subject or move on.

Since you are a part of a different culture, you should follow the host's lead and refrain from making certain gestures. The "thumbs up" sign may mean that plans are moving forward, but a client may take the phrase and imitation as insulting.

CHAPTER 22

Professional Communication and Technology

BUSINESS EMAIL COMMUNICATION

You should always respond to a real message within about the same amount of time as returning a telephone call. Twenty-four to forty-eight hours is good. This goes for an invitation to a meeting or a hello from an old friend. Junk mail and forwards don't necessarily need a response. If you take longer, be sure to acknowledge the delay and apologize.

Use the subject line to alert the receiver to the subject matter of your message. Grab their attention. When the subject matter of the email changes, be sure to change your subject line. This way, they'll read your message quickly, and you're more likely to get a faster response.

Leave all personal information out of email while at work and keep it professional. This isn't the venue for bad-mouthing coworkers or going on and on about your hot date over the weekend.

Select the correct recipients. Only the most relevant messages should be sent to all recipients. (Use the "Reply to All" tab responsibly.)

Mind your addresses. When sending out an email to a long list of recipients, it's best to use an address book function that doesn't list all recipients in the "To" header. You can type your own email address in the "To" line and "BCC" is a good way to avoid showing everyone's email address.

Watch your language. It's best to always reread your messages before sending them to make sure there are no grammatical or spelling errors. Avoid using slang language and email shorthand in business correspondence.

Use vocabulary that conveys professionalism. When responding to business requests, it's important to strike the right tone. While "I would love to" is warm and enthusiastic, it can sometimes sound overly casual depending on the setting. Here are a few alternatives that still express positivity and professionalism with a bit more polish.

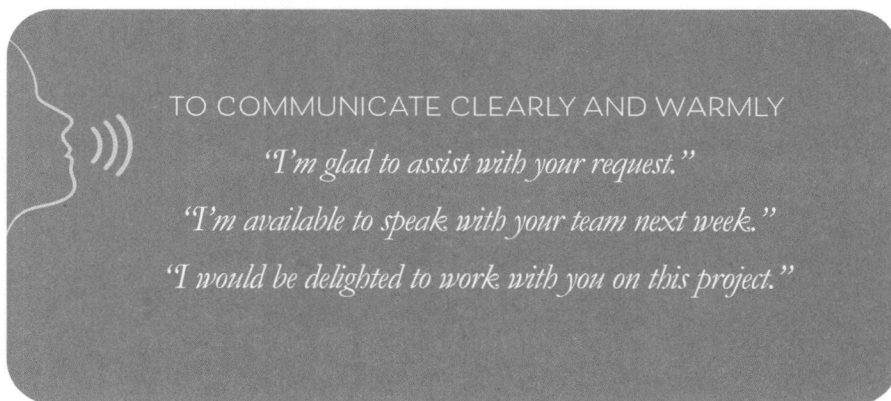

> TO COMMUNICATE CLEARLY AND WARMLY
>
> *"I'm glad to assist with your request."*
>
> *"I'm available to speak with your team next week."*
>
> *"I would be delighted to work with you on this project."*

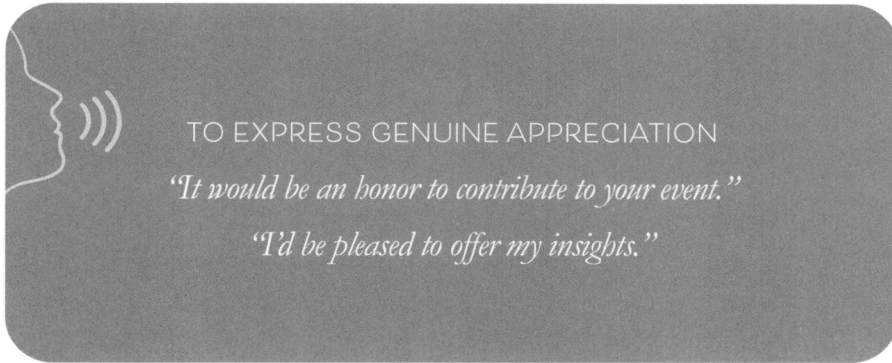

TO EXPRESS GENUINE APPRECIATION

"It would be an honor to contribute to your event."

"I'd be pleased to offer my insights."

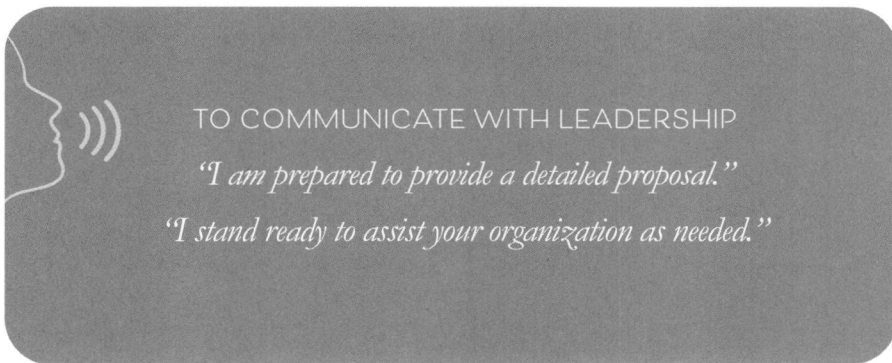

TO COMMUNICATE WITH LEADERSHIP

"I am prepared to provide a detailed proposal."

"I stand ready to assist your organization as needed."

Don't overstep your boundaries. If you're sending out an email that is religious, political, or pornographic, be sure to know that your intended recipient wants to receive it. Always adhere to company guidelines if you are sending messages from work and be prepared to deal with the consequences if you violate them.

Respond in a timely manner. Timely responses show respect and professionalism. Even if you don't have a full answer right away, acknowledge receipt of the email and let the sender know when they can expect a complete reply. Ideally, respond within twenty-four to forty-eight hours during business days.

Use exclamation points sparingly. While an exclamation point can convey friendliness and enthusiasm, overusing them can make your message seem overly casual or unprofessional. Limit yourself to one, if any, and reserve it for moments where genuine excitement is appropriate—such as congratulations or warm greetings.

Refrain from sending one-liners. Short replies like "Thanks" or "Okay" can sometimes come across as abrupt or dismissive. If you must send a brief response, try to add a touch of warmth or context. For example, instead of just "Thanks," you might say, "Thanks so much for sending this over!"

Keep it clean. Emails are professional documents. Avoid slang, emojis (unless appropriate for the relationship and situation), and especially anything that could be viewed as offensive, sarcastic, or inappropriate. Always reread your message before sending to ensure it maintains a polished, respectful tone.

Pick up the phone. If an email conversation starts to go back and forth without resolution, or if the topic is sensitive or complicated, it's often better to call. A phone call can prevent miscommunications, save time, and allow for a more nuanced conversation.

Don't use ALL CAPITAL LETTERS. Typing in all caps feels aggressive and is often interpreted as shouting. If you need to emphasize a word or phrase, use bold, italics, or simply rephrase your sentence for clarity instead of resorting to all caps.

PROPER TELEPHONE MANNERS

- When making calls, always identify yourself and your company.

- Quickly explain why you are calling.

- If you dial the wrong number, don't hang up. Just admit it and apologize.

- Ask the person if you can place them on hold rather than telling them you will place them on hold. Be sure to wait for them to respond.

- Let the person know before you put them on speakerphone.

- If others are present, be sure to make introductions.

- While on the phone, don't:
  o Eat

  o Chew gum

  o Multi-task

  o Blow your nose or sneeze directly into the receiver

- Always speak in a pleasant manner. Use kind phrases such as:
  o May I ask who is calling, please?

  o May I ask what this is in reference to, please?

- Tips for when you are speaking on the phone:
  o Keep your chin up when you talk.

  o Speak in a cheerful, pleasant, and upbeat manner.

  o Use correct vocabulary.

  o Speak in complete sentences.

  o Refrain from using slang language.

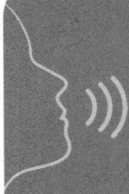

Here is how you would answer a call: "Thank you for calling The Swann School of Protocol. How may I help you?"

When the caller asks to speak with someone, your response can be one of these:

"I can see if he or she is available."

"May I ask who is calling, please?"

"May I ask what this is in reference to?"

"One moment, please. I will check and be right back with you." (Always use the hold button.)

If the individual is not available:

"Mr./Ms. is not available at this time. May I take a message?"

Write down the person's name, number, and message.

Repeat the information written down.

"Very well. I will be sure to pass this on as soon as he or she is available. Thank you for calling. Goodbye."

If the individual is available:

"Thank you for holding Mr./Ms. _____. One moment. I am going to transfer you now."

VIDEO CONFERENCING ETIQUETTE

- Ensure that you have a clean, presentable background.

- Try to attend the meeting from a space that is quiet, with minimal background movement and noise.

- Using the virtual background feature is acceptable. Additionally, it is an easy way to eliminate background distractions. You can use this when you have to meet in a messy or busy location.

- Mute your microphone while the presenter is speaking. This will keep background noise to a minimum.

- If your microphone is not muted, be sure to avoid doing activities that could create additional noise, such as opening wrappers or shuffling papers.

- Position your camera properly. It should be eye level. This helps create a more direct sense of engagement with other participants.

- Avoid multitasking. No texting, checking email, working on other projects, or using the phone unless it has something to do with the conversation at hand.

- Keep the camera on unless you have to step away. It is best not to walk away leaving an empty space. Send a quick note to the leader or follow any directions they may give on being excused for a moment.

- Don't walk around with the phone, tablet, or laptop. Too much movement can be very distracting.

- Don't shout. The microphone system is designed to pick up sound easily, so speak in your normal tone of voice.

- Keep body movement and hand gestures to a minimum.

- Don't interrupt others during the session. Instead, raise your hand.

- Don't carry on side conversations. Mute your microphone if you have to make a very brief statement to someone else in the room.

- Dress appropriately for the occasion.

- Do not snack or eat during the session. Sipping a beverage is acceptable, but be mindful of how you look and how it sounds.

- Log on early if you are the host so you can be prepared to receive people and take care of any possible technical difficulties.

- Always start on time and don't keep people waiting while you are waiting for others to come in. It's always important to honor the people who are present rather than waiting for late arrivals.

- You should honor people's time by ending at the appropriate time. If you feel or see that you're going to go over time, stop at the initial time and give people the option to bow out of the meeting or either let people know exactly how much more time you'll be going over and then you can continue.

- Be sure that you send out the proper notice ahead of time, including the link and sign-in information. If you have to update that information, be sure it is accurate.

- Reminders are always helpful, especially if you scheduled your meeting far in advance. You don't necessarily have to do this for meetings that are regular. Let's say, for example, you meet every Monday at a specific time. There's no need to send a reminder.

- Keep time zones in mind. People are all over, in multiple areas and countries, so be mindful of it. If you have to inconvenience yourself slightly so that you get connected with a person at their optimum time frame, then do so.

- If you get an invitation to a video conference and it's a platform that you haven't used before, take a little bit of time to familiarize yourself with it and the settings.

- If you are hosting a meeting and you're using a platform that is not mainstream, be prepared to assist attendees if necessary.

PROPER INTERNET USE AT WORK

- Saying "I didn't know" is not an excuse when it comes to internet and computer etiquette at work. Make it your business to know the company rules.

- Even if you spend a lot of hours at your job, you should only surf the web, shop online, or pay bills if the company permits you to do so. Keep time limits to a minimum.

- Rather than rely on your memory, keep a log of personal time spent online in the event you are questioned later.

- If questionable, certain websites you visit during your personal time and on your personal computer should not be the same ones you visit while at work.

- Remember, email accounts at work are not private. That email address does not belong to you personally; it's the company's email address. They have total rights to your account.

- Always project professionalism in correspondence. Watch your language.

- Be mindful of the information you share with others. Even if it's someone you know well, avoid sending out emails that are religious, political, or pornographic.

SOCIAL MEDIA AND BUSINESS

- The way we engage on social media for business can be very different from the way it is used for personal use. It is important to keep in mind the different ways we communicate between the two and remember the boundaries that separate what is and is not appropriate.

- Make sure you familiarize yourself with the company guidelines for social media behavior and your online presence.

- Keep in mind that nothing is ever really deleted from the internet. This means you are making a digital footprint in every space you manage.

- A private page doesn't really mean it's private. People can take a screenshot of what you have posted and share it with others.

- There are websites that can catalog old information from the internet.

- A good gauge to use is if you won't do it or say it in person, then don't do it or say it online.

- Get permission before you post other people's images online.

- Think twice before sharing photos of anything that has to do with your company, your employer, your coworkers, or any sensitive company information.

- Don't post information that could conflict with your resume.

- Don't be guilty by association. Be mindful of whom you connect with, what comments you like, and what photos you like. This includes things you might share or repost.

- Know when to "go pro." This means some online business relationships should only exist on a professional platform such as LinkedIn.

- It's perfectly fine to NOT accept an invitation to connect. Use the feature the social media platform offers to allow you to decline the invite.

KEY POINTS ABOUT DIGITALLY CONNECTING WITH CLIENTS AND COLLEAGUES

In this digital age, where emails and social media posts are primary ways to communicate, it seems that etiquette can get a little lost in the shuffle. Should you choose to connect with people via social media, recognize that you still represent your business, company, or brand. In business, it is most important to follow professional protocol when connecting online.

The proper structure of an email is important. Regardless of length, it should always include a salutation, body, and sign-off. It is inappropriate to start a business email off using slang language such as "Hey." Instead, use "Greetings," "Hello," or "Good morning/afternoon." When you close your email, sign off by using phrases such as "Kind regards," "Best wishes," or "Sincerely." The sign-off "Cheers" works well for friendly business relationships.

As mentioned earlier, it's always smart to "go pro" before going personal. If the relationship grows, you can consider connecting on more casual platforms.

There is no golden rule that says all friend requests on personal platforms like Facebook must be accepted. You can ignore a colleague's request. If they mention it later, you can say something simple like, "I reserve Facebook for family members only, but how about we connect on LinkedIn?" Your goal is to let them know that your negative response was nothing personal.

Since X (formerly Twitter) is an open forum, it is perfectly fine to follow colleagues on this platform. It gives you the opportunity to keep up with them from a more casual perspective, and you can also send them a direct message as another means of contact.

BUSINESS AND TECH (PRIORITIZING FACE-TO-FACE VS. DIGITAL COMMUNICATION)

You are getting ready to close the deal with a high-profile client when your phone vibrates. You have been expecting an email from another client all day, and this may be the golden message that you have been anticipating. Should you take two seconds away from your in-person meeting to check your email? No, you should not. Stay present and give your full attention to the person in front of you.

FACE-TO-FACE OVERRIDES ONLINE

No email should take priority over someone who's made time to speak with you in person. Responding, or even reading, your email while in a meeting with someone else, especially a VIP, is the equivalent of sporadically starting a conversation with a random bystander without concluding the discussion at hand.

STAYING CONNECTED IS IMPERATIVE

You cannot properly interact with the person in front of you while responding to an email or text message. Giving full attention to the associate standing before you is essential to good business and success. Of course, emergencies are exceptions to the rule, and if you MUST take another call, be open and clear and let your present party know at the start that you MAY have to accept a quick call so there are no surprises. Make sure all parties are in agreement beforehand. Otherwise, let the call wait.

CHAPTER 23

Job Interviews and Career Advancement

JOB INTERVIEW ETIQUETTE

Good grooming is essential. Create a good foundation. No outfit is stylish without good grooming. Your basic hygiene is most vital. Fingernails should be neat and clean. If you wear acrylic nails they should be properly filled. Nail polish should be worn completely on or completely off, not chipped. Hair should be clean and styled in a classic manner. Avoid overbearing lotions, perfumes, and colognes.

Research the company before the interview. It's important to do your homework on the company prior to the interview. Be sure you understand what the company is all about. Do some research and pull some articles about the company to find out how you would fit in. You'll likely get asked, "What could you do for this company?" Be sure that you have an answer to it.

Dress appropriately for the position. This may take some research. Find out the expected dress code, whether it's traditional office wear, business casual, or casual.

The traditional power colors black, blue, gray, and brown are still acceptable and highly recommended. Avoid wearing jeans. Even if the job is one where you normally would wear jeans, opt for a pair of tan khakis and a nice polo type shirt instead. Make sure your shoes are neat and clean.

Choose a trim resume holder along with a pen and pad of paper. Don't load yourself down with a bunch of stuff. Know in advance if you need to bring samples of your work or additional materials. If so, then pack light and simple. Choose something in black, brown, or burgundy that is easy to reach into without causing a fuss during the interview. Be sure you bring a pen and paper along to take notes.

Get directions. Make sure you have the correct directions. Use Google Maps to get correct driving directions. Call in advance and double-check with the receptionist if necessary. Leave your house with enough time to allow for unexpected delays.

Arrive on time. On time means fifteen minutes early. It's better for you to wait than to be waited on. Once you arrive, give yourself a "once-over." Check yourself one last time for any imperfections, leave your cell phone in silent mode, pop a mint in your mouth, and head on in.

Be polite to everyone. Greet the receptionist with a pleasant "Good Morning," or "Good Afternoon," then say, "My name is (first and last name) and I have a three o'clock appointment with Ms. Sequoia Gorham." If the receptionist is on the telephone, don't interrupt. Wait patiently until they're finished with the call. Remember, you're there early so you can wait.

Greet with a firm handshake and maintain good eye contact during the interview. Once you are called in for the interview, greet your interviewer by keeping it simple.

Just stand up straight, smile, say their name, and give them a firm handshake. It's a good idea to practice shaking hands at home. Avoid handshakes that are too limp or overpowering.

Pay attention to your body language. Stand and sit up straight; don't slouch. Don't stare the interviewer in the eyes too hard; just make sure your eyes meet frequently. Be moderate in talking with your hands and using hand gestures.

Be mindful of how you hand over resumes and portfolios. During the interview, if you have materials or a portfolio to present, wait until the interviewer has asked to review it. Be sure to open it up and turn it towards the interviewer, allowing them to read it from their direction.

Mind your voice and vocabulary. Speak clearly and audibly, not too softly nor too loudly. Be sure you make good use of the English language. Avoid using slang words and know your vocabulary before you use it. If the industry you are applying for uses specific jargon, you may want to include some as you answer questions. You give the interviewer a chance to hear you speak like one of their team members.

Keep conversation pleasant and professional. Don't go on and on about yourself. Don't talk too much or too little. Avoid making demands about pay, benefits, or perks. Don't become so comfortable to where you wind up sounding like you're just shooting the breeze with your friends.

Leave a lasting impression. At the end of the interview, stand, make eye contact, give a firm handshake, and thank the interviewer for their time. Follow up with a brief thank-you note by email or traditional mail.

CHAPTER 24

Business Faux Pas and How to Recover

We have all been there. We've all been in the middle of a meeting or social gathering and made a huge mistake in mannerism. While some of us froze in our tracks, a few of us tried to move on to no avail. Here are four of the most common mistakes in business etiquette and how you can recover from them.

MISTAKE #1: IMPROPER GESTURES

While it is true that your friends know that the "okay" sign means that all is well, a business partner from another country or culture may not view the gesture as a good thing. In fact, hand motions like the "okay" sign and "thumbs up" are quite offensive in some nations. The best way to recover from an improper hand gesture is to ask for a pardon and provide an explanation. Most international partners will understand variations in culture and are willing to forgive such errors. Just see to it that you don't use them anymore while on the trip.

MISTAKE #2: JOKES THAT GO SOUTH

You may find the story hilarious, but your guests do not. You can always tell when a joke hits a soft spot in conference settings because of the dead silence and motions of discomfort that attendees give. Should you tell a joke that is less than humorous during business meetings, do yourself a favor and do not continue. Instead, act as if you never presented the joke and move the conversation along. Consider doing something selfless for the offended party if you have severed a relationship beyond the initial meeting.

MISTAKE #3: ADDRESSING COLLEAGUES WITH THE WRONG TITLE

This is why it is so important to follow the lead of your host. They know their superior's ranking and will never leave you out to dry when introducing you to them. As a rule of thumb, it is always appropriate to address a person by their last name in a business setting. You should refrain from referring to an individual by their first name unless they give you permission to do so. Simply correct your mistake if you happen to call a colleague by his first name during a conference.

MISTAKE #4: USING SLANG LANGUAGE

"That's a no-brainer." Come again? Most North Americans know that this phrase signifies a task being easy to complete. Individuals from other countries, however, may view such a statement as an insult. Immediately explain what a phrase means if you accidentally use slang and move forward with the understanding that directly conversing with colleagues is necessary in international business settings.

HOW TO TURN A "WEIRD" BUSINESS CONVERSATION AROUND

It's the moment that makes you squirm. You're in mid-conversation with a coworker, friend, or business associate when the camaraderie becomes debatable. Somewhere between the laughs, they said something that you really don't agree with. It may have changed "business" to "personal" or may have been somewhat offensive. Now the air has left the room, and tensions are getting high. So how do you change the subject?

HOW TO SHIFT AN AWKWARD CONVERSATION

- Turn awkwardness into something interesting. They may have asked a silly or inappropriate question, and now there is a bit of bitterness in the atmosphere. Turn "lemons into lemonade" by quickly posing another inquiry to another subject.

- Focus on them. Or, instead of coming out of left field with a brand-new question, base your inquisitiveness off their life. Let them talk about their accomplishments and listen for cues where you can jump in and change the subject.

- Take advantage of vacations and hobbies. Their trip to Spain is a prime opportunity for you to turn the conversation into something more pleasurable. Ask them to give details about the sights so that they are less inclined to reference an awkward subject.

PART FIVE

Digital World Etiquette

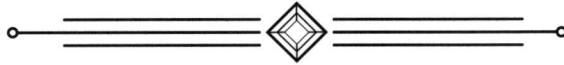

THRIVING WITH GRACE IN
A CONNECTED WORLD

The digital world moves fast, but etiquette helps us slow down long enough to be kind.

- ELAINE SWANN -

CHAPTER 25

Cell Phone Etiquette

The digital world moves fast, but etiquette helps us slow down long enough to be kind. Technology has made us more connected than ever, but at the same time we are sometimes disconnected. It makes it easier for us to forget our manners. So, in this section, we'll explore the new rules of engagement for our digital lives. We'll talk about dealing with texting so that we don't offend, sending an email with clarity, taking a video conference like a pro, and how to maintain a positive image on social media. These guidelines aren't about being rigid; they're about showing up as your very best self even when you are behind the screen. Because in the virtual world, courtesy still counts.

THE RIGHT TIME TO REACH OUT

When it comes to calls, text messages, and FaceTime, be mindful of the time of day and the time zone that the person is in. My recommendation is to use the nine-to-nine strategy: no calls or text messages before 9:00 in the morning.

Avoid making calls or sending text messages after 9:00 in the evening. Don't do this unless you know the person very well or you've made a promise. For example, you were out, and they asked you to text them to let them know once you got home. Or if you're meeting up with them and it's an early, before 9:00 am sort of thing. Other than that, my recommendation is to use the nine-to-nine strategy.

FACETIME RULES

FaceTime is more intimate than a regular phone call, so give the person a heads-up before you dial in. Also, make sure that you are in a quiet space and you're aware of your surroundings because people don't want to be dragged into a FaceTime call that is noisy or messy. You also don't want to overshare your personal information while you're on video. Be camera ready. Keep in mind when you FaceTime, it's almost like opening your front door and letting someone in, so you want to make sure that your appearance is appropriate. And finally, do not screenshot your call without the other person's permission. Remember, this is a more intimate manner of communication.

PROPER CELL PHONE ETIQUETTE

The person standing face-to-face with you has top priority. It's rude to leave the person you are with feeling less important than the caller.

Keep your private matters private. No one wants to hear the most intimate aspects of your life.

Speak softly. Nothing is more annoying than listening to someone's loud, brash conversation.

Respect the personal space of others. Try to keep a good ten-foot distance between you and others. Don't keep people trapped in your space, such as on an elevator or bank line.

If you can't talk, don't answer. It is rude to answer a call only to immediately tell a person you are preoccupied. Instead, let the call go to voicemail and return the call when you are available.

Know when to silence your phone completely. Worship service, weddings, funerals, the waiting room of the doctor's office, movie theaters, and enclosed public places are off limits.

Be wary of novelty ringtones, and use the vibrate function often. Not everyone wants to hear some pop star's latest hit while you search for your phone as it vibrates against the tin can of mints in your bag or pocket.

When wearing earbuds and talking in public, be mindful of the volume of your voice and how you direct it towards others. Nothing's more confusing than a person walking towards you, ranting out loud with their earpiece in, and you think they're ranting to you or just plain crazy.

For your safety, if you must use your phone for an extended time and you feel yourself becoming distracted while driving, pull over.

Use your phone's features, such as voicemail, caller ID, and text messaging. This way, you'll never miss an important message, you'll know exactly who's calling, and you can send a brief message without interrupting the party you are with.

When dining, do not place your phone on the dinner table. Place it in your pocket or bag. Nothing should go on top of the table except for food and beverage.

When dining, it is acceptable to take a photo of your meal or with your party if it is a social occasion. However, wait until later to post it to social media. This way, you remain engaged with the people you are with.

When dining with others, only use your phone if it has something to do with the conversation at hand. For example, you may look up movie times and share with your party or send a text to someone you are waiting on.

I have shared this before: if you have to take a phone call, move away from others and take the call privately.

PROPER CELL PHONE ETIQUETTE WHEN YOU'RE IN SOMEONE'S HOUSE

When you're at someone's home, before you start posting with your phone and taking pictures or videos, make sure you get permission first, especially if you're featuring a certain background. There might be family photos, artwork, artifacts, rugs, furniture, or sentimental items. Or, sometimes, the background might not be as tidy as the host prefers. You don't want to take someone's home and put it on the internet without their permission. It only takes a quick moment to say, "Hey, is it okay if I use this background?" If they say yes, great. If not, then don't. And if you're ever not sure, then it's probably a no.

GROUP CHATS AND TEXT THREADS

Group chats can really be helpful, fun, and in some instances they are quite necessary, especially when it comes to family, but sometimes they can become overwhelming if you don't handle them properly. Keep in mind whether it's your family or coworkers and be mindful of how often you are sending messages, and don't spam people with back-to-back texts. Try to keep your information succinct, so don't take something that can be used as one complete sentence and break it up into three or four text messages. It is absolutely fine for you to leave the chat if it no longer serves a purpose or if you just don't want to be in it. You can send a message saying, "Thanks, everyone. I'm going to step out of the thread now. Keep me posted if anything different comes up." You don't have to give a big explanation and go into a great amount of detail. Be kind as you leave the chat.

VOICE NOTES AND AUDIO MESSAGES

Sending a voice note is very convenient, but keep in mind that your timing and context really matter. Typically, you want to use a voice note when a text message is too long to type or when your tone is important. Technology does not transfer tone well, so sometimes people need to hear your voice in order to convey your message clearly, but keep your voice message short and sweet. Don't go on and on. Try to keep it under a minute. If it takes longer than that, then just call the person. Also, don't leave a voice note when you know that a person is not in an area or space where they can freely listen to the message. Sometimes people are at work or in a quiet environment, so it's best to avoid sending a voice note when they may not be able to listen right away.

EMAIL ETIQUETTE ON MOBILE DEVICES

There's a difference between emailing a person and texting them. In text messaging there's shorthand that you can use, but in an email, especially in a business environment, you should still use proper communication skills and be mindful of your tone. Add an additional note at the signature line of your email that says something to let the reader know that it's being sent from your phone to excuse any typos but don't just rely on that. Take a look at what you have written before you send it.

SCREEN TIME AND PUBLIC DEVICE USE

It's important to be aware of how often and how long you are looking at your screen. Be mindful of this, especially when you're in the presence of others. Whether you are at a restaurant, family gathering, or even a social event, constant scrolling tends to send a message that you're not fully present. When people are face-to-face with you, they have top priority. If you need to check your phone, do it briefly. On public transportation, use earbuds and be mindful of how bright the screen is in places such as movie theaters. When you're mindful, you show respect for others.

CHAPTER 26

Social Media Etiquette

SOCIAL MEDIA TAGGING AND SHARING

Always get permission before you post somebody's photo on social media. They may not want to have this photo shared online. It only takes a second to ask. So, the moment you take that photo, turn to the individual and ask them, "Is it okay if I post this?" It's also a good idea to ask someone's permission before you tag them in a social media post, especially if you do not know them well. With some social media platforms, when you tag them, it means that your image is going to show up on their feed, and they may not want that. There's a difference between tagging people who are your friends and you're sharing. But if it's someone you don't know well, get permission first.

RESPECTING PRIVACY ON PERSONAL MILESTONES

It is important to recognize that not every person wants to share all of their personal milestones, so if they ask you to take something down that you've shared, then be respectful and simply take it down. We all have a different perspective on how much we share about ourselves, but certain people prefer to keep personal milestones quiet, and it's important that we respect that.

FOUNDATIONS OF ONLINE COURTESY

- Be authentic when you are online. Misleading others may lead to your own harm.

- Limit what you say and upload. Resist the urge to share too much information about you, your family, and your friends.

- Bullying on the internet is the same as bullying in person.

- Do not post pictures or share information that shows your friends or family in an unflattering way.

- If you don't have something nice to say, don't say anything at all.

- Keep in mind that nothing is ever really deleted from the internet.

- People can take a screenshot of what you have posted and share it with others.

- Some websites can catalog old information from the internet.

- Don't say mean things to or about other people online.

- Get permission before you post other people's images online.

- Get permission first before taking photos or videos in people's homes.

- It is perfectly fine to untag yourself or unfollow a friend or follower on a social media site.

BUILDING A POSITIVE DIGITAL REPUTATION

Every once in a while, you should do a clean sweep of your page. This means you should go through your page and review what you have posted, liked, commented on, and shared. It is important to do this because you can face repercussions based on these factors. It's perfectly acceptable to decline an invitation to connect. Use the technology that the social media platform has provided for you. Whether it is the "ignore" or "delete request" button, each platform gives you a way to reject a request. Don't feel pressured to give a reason or explanation. Know when to "Go Pro." Some online relationships should exist only on a professional platform such as LinkedIn or Alignable.

WHAT TO POST ON PROFESSIONAL PLATFORMS

On sites like LinkedIn, your posts should reflect your professional life and values. This can include sharing industry news, celebrating work milestones, offering thought leadership, promoting your own professional achievements, or uplifting others in your field. Avoid overly personal updates or anything that could be considered divisive or off-brand for your career. When in doubt, ask: "*Would I share this in a team meeting or professional conference?*"

THE TWO P'S OF SOCIAL MEDIA:

You may remember the Two P's of Social Media from earlier: Post and Pose. They apply just as importantly to our personal lives as they do to professional settings. So, be mindful of them both:

Post: Don't post photos that could be offensive to others. Avoid sharing images that show yourself or your loved ones in a negative light. Never post photos that make fun of or harm someone else, even if you do not know them.

Pose: Be mindful of how you pose with friends, at parties, on vacations, and at social gatherings. Remember that photos can last forever online, so always pose in a way that reflects positively on you and those around you.

WHEN POSTS HAVE CONSEQUENCES

Even in your private life, what you post on social media can have professional repercussions. Employers, clients, and colleagues often view personal social media activity as a reflection of your judgment and character.

Many individuals have lost their jobs or faced serious consequences because of what they shared online. And in some instances, they were posts they thought were harmless at the time.

WHEN A BAD SOCIAL MEDIA POST LED TO REAL CONSEQUENCES

A university student named Connie L. took a part-time job at a clothing store. Hoping to sound supportive of her clientele, she posted on Facebook:

"Conquering the world, one well-dressed fat lady at a time."

Her manager didn't see it that way. The comment was viewed as disrespectful toward customers, and Connie was fired immediately.

SHARING PHOTOS RESPECTFULLY

If you snap a photo of a friend, get permission BEFORE you post their picture on your social media page. It only takes a second to ask.

With social media pictures and posts, keep in mind that as you share personal moments of your own life, you don't expose the intimate details of another person's life.

If you won't show it or say it in person, then don't show it or say it online.

Have fun taking pictures while you enjoy your time with others. It's best to wait until later to post them up on your social media page. You don't want to be distracted by continually looking at comments and interacting with others online. It is best to simply live in the moment.

DM ETIQUETTE

When reaching out via DM (Direct Message), especially on a professional platform like LinkedIn, it's important to be respectful and professional. If you don't know the individual, introduce yourself. State your purpose and keep it brief. Don't drone on and on. If you find that you've sent multiple messages and the person hasn't responded, then it's likely they won't and perhaps you should try another way. Serious business requests should be taken to email as opposed to a DM. In a personal space, be mindful of sending people a direct message that you don't know. Keep in mind that some of the social media platforms don't necessarily send your message directly to their inbox, so one good thing to do is to send your message and then on the front of the platform page in a comment section just let the person know that you sent them a DM. This can alert them to your message. It's a great way to let the person know to check that other inbox.

GUARDING YOUR MIND AGAINST ONLINE NEGATIVITY

Have you ever found yourself going back and forth with someone over email or text, and the conversation starts to get intense? If you want to protect your mind, your sight, and your spirit, the answer is simple: Don't read it. Don't open it. Leave it unread. Don't even allow it to enter your spirit. I can tell you from experience, there was a time when someone sent me a message, and I knew it was not going to be good. So, you know what I did? I didn't even read it. As a result, I have no memory of it. It's not in my spirit and not in my mind. I have no idea what they said because I made the decision to stop and not let it into my space. I want you to do the same. Stop negativity in its tracks and push it away.

CHAPTER 27

Virtual Meeting Etiquette

Note: For a full guide on virtual meeting etiquette in professional settings, see the Professional Communication and Technology section. The tips below focus on everyday virtual gatherings and casual meetings.

Don't be "doin' stuff." Doing things such as having side conversations with other people in the room, making big sweeping movements that are clearly not intended for the meeting, and overly multitasking is rude and can detract from the meeting.

Do beverages the right way. Etiquette would dictate that it is absolutely acceptable to have a beverage while you are having a virtual meeting. Just be mindful of a few things.

Coffee mugs are acceptable. Be mindful of any messaging on the cup that can be viewed as offensive. Try to avoid plastic disposable bottles. There's nothing more distracting than people having to watch you and hearing a sucking sound and crushing a bottle as you turn your head up, taking in that last drop of water.

Resist the urge to snack and eat on camera. Even with the sound off, it can be distracting.

Do set yourself up to be respected by your peers. Because such a high percentage of people feel it's rude to turn your camera off, don't put yourself in the category of an individual who would not be respected by other attendees. Having that camera off may give off a voyeurism type of vibe and can even feel creepy when you are speaking up yet are unseen. Turning your camera on tells the others that you are present and engaged in the meeting and the discussion at hand.

BEING RESPECTFUL OF NOISE LEVELS

Not muting yourself and having background noise are considered to be the rudest things someone can do during a virtual meeting. It's annoying, distracting, and downright rude to allow noise from your personal environment to seep into a virtual meeting. It's similar to standing outside of a conference room with the door open and carrying on a loud conversation. Close the virtual door and mute your audio.

ATTENDING THE LIVESTREAM OF A WEDDING

Consider offering some distant friends and family the option to attend a wedding or special occasions via a video platform. People have found value in the ability to include loved ones who live far distances away to take part in their special day.

Get Dressed and Look the Part

You don't necessarily have to mimic everyone who's there in person. But for the most part, get dressed, do your hair. Add a bit of makeup if you feel like it. This is a sacred occasion, and the way you show up should be treated as such.

Turn the Camera On

You want to fully take part in this moment in time and show the couple that you are present for their special day. Having a black screen can make it feel a bit voyeuristic.

Be Mindful of Your Surroundings and Background

Just like you would tidy up before guests come to your home, take a moment to clean up your background. Sit in a quiet space with good lighting and avoid distractions like loud TVs or other people walking behind you. This shows respect for the couple and the moment they've invited you to witness.

Treat It Like a Real Ceremony, Because It Is

Even though you're tuning in virtually, don't multitask during the ceremony. Put your phone down, stop scrolling, and give the couple your full attention. Just like you wouldn't chat through someone's vows in person, you want to be fully present during their special moment.

GIVE THE GIFT OF A VIRTUAL EXPERIENCE

As we move into seeing more entertainment delivered on digital platforms, think about personalizing a gift for a family member or loved one that really taps into their personal likes and interests. This is the epitome of gift-giving. The great thing about giving the gift of a virtual experience is that the person can enjoy it in the presence of their own home, safe from uncomfortable elements such as weather, traffic, parking, and crowds.

ZOOM FATIGUE AND VIDEO CALL BOUNDARIES

Zoom fatigue" is a term people use to describe the mental exhaustion that comes from too many video calls, especially when you're expected to stay visually engaged the entire time. It is absolutely acceptable to ask for a phone call instead of a video call. There are some conversations that absolutely need to be on camera. Alternatively, there are instances where they don't, or there might be a time when you're just feeling a bit overwhelmed or drained by constant video calls. If this happens, it is perfectly acceptable to ask the individual to take a phone call instead. This is especially true if the topic doesn't require face-to-face interaction or screen sharing for your discussion. You can simply say, "Would you be open to a phone call for this meeting?" Be honest with them. You can also add, "I'm trying to give my eyes a break from a screen for now." Most people will appreciate your honesty, and in some cases, they might even feel the same way.

MUTING AND UNMUTING ETIQUETTE

It's important to know how to manage your microphone during meetings or webinars. If you're not speaking, then keep yourself on mute. The only time you would not do this is if you are fully engaged in an ongoing discussion where your rapid response is necessary. The reason you want to mute your microphone is to avoid any background noises, interruptions, or unexpected distractions that can take place on your end. This is especially important in larger meetings or webinars. It is very intrusive to have unexpected noise happening and people can't tell where it is coming from. Whenever it is your turn to talk, simply unmute and speak clearly. It's a good practice to unmute your microphone just before it's your moment to speak. If you accidentally talk while muted just smile, unmute, and pick up where you left off. There's no need to go into detail and apologize profusely and make it awkward for everybody else. Using good mic etiquette keeps the flow of virtual meetings with people respectful of everyone involved.

VIRTUAL BACKGROUNDS AND FILTERS

Know when fun backgrounds are appropriate and when they are not. Some virtual backgrounds and filters can be a fun way to show your personality, but keep in mind that they're not always the right fit for the right time. If you're in a casual meeting or a social call with your friends or family, it's alright to have fun with them. But if you are taking a more formal meeting such as one with a client, a job interview, or you are doing a professional presentation, it's best to keep your background clean and as neutral as possible. You can utilize a solid image such as a logo and that can work well to represent your brand. If you have a very busy background area and you don't want to show it, you can blur it. That function is acceptable in business and causal settings. The key here is you want people to focus on what you're saying and not the tropical beach behind you.

CHAPTER 28
Digital Decorum

CHARGING STATIONS AND EV ETIQUETTE

More and more people are relying on the shared resources of a vehicle charging station. It's important to display common courtesy. Charging station spaces are shared spaces, not personal parking spots. Once your vehicle is fully charged, be sure to move it right away so someone else can plug in. Don't leave your car parked in the spot longer than necessary, even if the station isn't crowded when you arrive. You can simply monitor your app or your dashboard or set a reminder for yourself so you can unplug within a timely manner.

SMART HOME DEVICES (ALEXA, GOOGLE HOME, ETC.)

It's a good idea to mute your smart devices during meetings or gatherings. If you are hosting a professional call or a social get-together, mute or turn off devices such as Alexa or Google Home. Accidental activations can interrupt the flow of the moment and make people feel uncomfortable. Do your best to put others at ease so they don't feel as if they have to temper their conversation.

IN-HOME SECURITY CAMERAS

If you have indoor security cameras that record audio or video, there may be some instances when you would want to let your guests know they are being recorded. You want people to feel comfortable in your home, and disclosing this information when needed can help achieve that. You can simply say, "Just so you know, we've got a couple of cameras inside for security."

You can also put a stylish welcome sign near the entrance of your home to let people know they're being recorded. If you're hosting a gathering and unable to greet every guest, a stylish welcome sign near the entrance can help ensure they're informed.

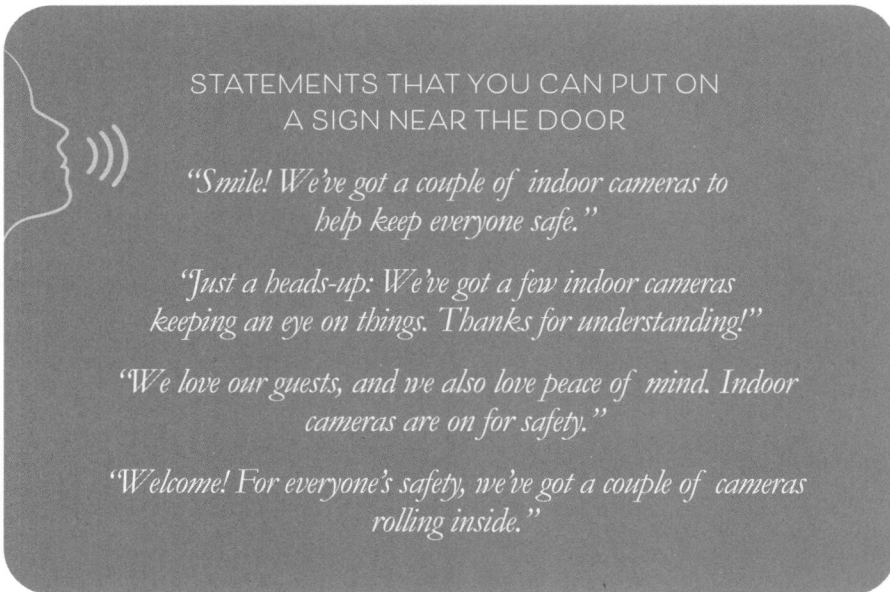

Keep in mind you don't always have to disclose this information. Use your discretion to determine when to share that cameras are present or when to turn them off altogether. Here is a breakdown of when to let guests know and when it is probably not necessary.

- If guests are staying overnight.
- When you are having a gathering where intimate information is being shared, such as a "girlfriend get-together" or when family affairs are being discussed.

When It Is Probably Not Necessary

- When service workers or contractors are present.
- For brief drop-ins or entryway visits.
- When the camera is clearly visible and in a standard area.

When you share this information in advance, it shows that you respect the individuals and allows them to adjust their behavior as needed.

COMMENTING AND ONLINE REVIEWS

Commenting online is definitely a resource that is necessary because online comments can help other people. Whether you're praising an establishment or service or warning others about it. But make sure that you're not doing so to tear somebody down or from a revenge perspective. You have to look at what your heart is saying about it. Think about how what you say is going to impact this business or individual. Make sure that you're always truthful about your experience and don't embellish. And if you always come from a perspective of wanting to help people, that will allow you to really share your thoughts from a purer perspective.

AI AND CHATBOT INTERACTIONS

As you navigate online, you'll see that a lot of companies are using AI and chatbots for their customer service. It's important to recognize when that's who you're talking to as you're corresponding. If the responses feel a bit generic and don't necessarily line up with your question, it's likely that you're dealing with AI. Be patient, be polite, and if you need more help, take a look around the website to see if there's another option to speak with or correspond with a real person. There's no need to be rude or get frustrated with a chatbot. It's not human.

So, adjust your expectations, do your best to communicate clearly, and get the support that you need.

POLITENESS AND PERSONALIZATION WITH AI

AI is a tool—not a replacement. We should use it to support our efforts in communicating with people, but not to substitute genuine interaction. When texting and emailing first became popular, I would always say that tone doesn't transfer well. And even though AI is smarter now, we still have to make sure we interject our tone and intent.

The best way to use AI is to explain what you want to communicate. For example, if you're writing a thank-you note, a professional email, or a social media post, be authentic. Share your thoughts and feelings. You might say: "I want to convey my heartfelt thanks. This person did something meaningful for me, and I want that gratitude to come through clearly." Then let the AI help you shape the message. Just make sure your own voice is leading the way.

In professional or academic settings, we must disclose when AI has been used—especially if guidelines are in place. Transparency is important.

And here's the big one: Convenience should never override connection.

AI can't be an excuse for being impersonal or careless. We already see how people hide behind screens and become brash or mean online. We can't let AI follow that same path. The language we teach AI should include kindness and care, even if it takes more effort or resources. I believe we can and should teach AI to be polite, but we have to model that behavior first.

We shouldn't turn kindness off and on. If we're using AI to communicate, we shouldn't be harsh or robotic in those interactions, then suddenly try to show up warm and polished in real life. That's like being rude and short with your family at home, then putting on a friendly face in public. Etiquette is also about consistency. If we want AI to be an extension of ourselves, then we should bring kindness into every space, including digital ones.

PART SIX

Money, Travel and Hosting

HANDLING LIFE'S DETAILS WITH
GENEROSITY, CARE, AND STYLE

Graciousness doesn't take a vacation; it travels with you, tips generously, and always writes a thank-you note.

- ELAINE SWANN -

CHAPTER 29

Money and Tipping Etiquette

Graciousness doesn't take a vacation; it travels with you, tips generously, and always writes a thank-you note. Graciousness can follow us everywhere, including the innermost parts of our lives. Whether you're booking a hotel, tipping at a restaurant, or hosting a guest in your home, the way you behave speaks volumes about your thoughtfulness toward others. This section covers money matters, travel etiquette, and the art of being a gracious host and a respectful guest. Because respect, honesty, and consideration aren't confined to special occasions—they are present in the way we manage even the smallest exchanges in our daily lives.

AVOIDING CONVERSATIONS ABOUT PERSONAL FINANCES

If you've lost your job or are experiencing financial struggles and don't want to talk about it, you don't have to. I talk about this in my book Let Crazy Be Crazy. Be direct and clear in your response.

If someone asks a question you don't want to answer, say, "That's not something I want to talk about," or "I'd rather not discuss that." Then, shift the conversation: "So, anyway, how was your vacation? I saw that you went to Honolulu for the third time. What was it like?"

You can prepare in advance by anticipating which family member will ask intrusive questions. Instead of dreading it, acknowledge that it will happen and plan your way out. Think about what topics the nosy relative enjoys discussing and use that as your pivot. That way, you're not caught off guard, and you remain in control of the conversation.

HOW TO POLITELY ASK FOR MONEY OWED TO YOU

It's perfectly acceptable to ask someone to return the money they owe you. The key is to be polite and direct without being too harsh. Say:

"Hey, just a reminder about the $50 from dinner the other night. Would you be able to send it this week?"

If the situation drags on, use my "Rule of Three" and follow up only twice more. You can say, "I'm checking in again to see when you might be able to send the money" or "Do you have an update yet on when you'll be able to send the money along?" After that, if they haven't paid, my recommendation is to move on and make a mental note that this is likely someone you should not loan to in the future.

DECLINING TO LEND MONEY TO FRIENDS OR FAMILY

Lending money to friends or family can complicate relationships. If you're not comfortable, it's perfectly fine to say no. Say:

"I'm not in a position to lend money right now,

but I hope things work out for you."

Or you can offer to help in another way. Another approach is to give what you can afford to lose and not expect anything back. For example, if someone asks for $100 and you can stand to lose $50, then give them $50.

Here's the bottom line: my advice is to never lend but to give and not expect it back. Setting these boundaries will help prevent resentment.

DECLINING TO JOIN EXPENSIVE PLANS

If you're invited to an expensive outing that doesn't fit your budget, decline politely and do it early. Say:

"I'd love to join, but it's not in my budget right now.

But I'd love to plan something else with you soon."

MONEY ETIQUETTE AND SOCIAL MEDIA: AVOID BRAGGING

It's considered poor taste to brag about money, purchases, or luxury experiences on social media. Sharing travel photos or life updates is fine, but flaunting wealth or showing off expensive gifts can come across as boastful. True etiquette calls for humility both in person and online.

DON'T ASK FOR MONEY ON SOCIAL MEDIA

Avoid posting your payment app handle on social media to ask for money on your birthday and special occasions. This includes asking for money for your children as well. If someone chooses to send you a monetary gift, it should be voluntary and thoughtful, not prompted by a public request. Social media isn't a gift registry, and your birthday isn't a fundraiser unless it's clearly tied to a charitable cause.

If you would really like to receive money for your birthday, let your close friends and family know privately and tie it to a personal goal. And if others choose to bless you unexpectedly, receive it with gratitude. But as a general rule: don't make your followers feel obligated to contribute just because it's your special day.

SPLITTING THE BILL AT A RESTAURANT

People often hesitate to talk about money, but a good approach is to address this early in your dining experience. You can ask your fellow diners before, or just as the server comes to take the order. You can say something as simple as:

"Hey folks, how are we going to split the bill?

Two and two? Four and four? Are we all paying evenly?"

This way, you can just sit back and enjoy the meal. You won't be distracted by figuring out how to take care of the bill the entire time you are eating.

Yes, it is acceptable to ask to pay separately. My recommendation is to bring it up the moment you sit down. Or you can bring it up when you are waiting to be seated at your table. Here are some specific questions to ask or statements to make:

"Hey there, what are we going to do? Are we paying separate bills?"

"Should we go ahead and do separate checks?"

"Just so we're clear for the server, would you prefer separate checks or one bill?"

"Do you mind if we do separate checks tonight? I'm trying to stick to a budget right now."

SPLITTING THE BILL WHEN CELEBRATING AN OCCASION

If you're the one who did the inviting and selected the restaurant, then you are responsible for paying. However, if everyone else collectively decides to celebrate you and you are the honored guest, the group should either split the bill evenly to cover your costs, or the host should pay for you. Bottom line: If you do the inviting, you pay. If they do the inviting, they pay.

WHEN YOU DIDN'T EAT AS MUCH AS EVERYONE ELSE

When dining with friends, it's not uncommon for the check to be split evenly, even if you only had a salad and water while others enjoyed entrées, appetizers, desserts, and wine. In situations like this, remember that the split often reflects the spirit of the gathering, not just the cost of your meal.

If you find yourself in this situation, you have a few options:

- Ask the server if it's possible to split the check individually.

- Speak to the group's ringleader and offer to contribute a little more toward the tip. It might cost more than you expected, but less than splitting the full bill evenly.

- Bite the bullet and split the check evenly. If you choose this, take it in stride, and next time, plan ahead by finding out how the group handles checks before you dine.

EVEN SPLITS IN HIGH-PROFILE DINING SITUATIONS

Now, in some instances, the check might be split evenly regardless of what you ordered. If you're in a high-profile setting—maybe with executives, celebrities, or a more affluent crowd—and the dining experience is elevated or exclusive, expect to split the check evenly. If you're in a private dining area, an exclusive club, or a fine dining restaurant where the chef comes out to greet you, you will likely split the check evenly. The experience is the focus, not what you personally ordered. If that doesn't fit your budget, that's just not the group you want to dine with on a regular basis.

TIPPING ETIQUETTE - THE OLD WORLD VS. THE NEW WORLD

The word "tip" is believed to come from early 18th-century British slang meaning "to give" or "to pass." In taverns and coffeehouses, patrons would tip servants a coin for faster service. There's also a popular story that the word stands for To Improve Prompt Service, often told in reference to tea gardens in the 1600s. However, linguists agree the slang origin is more accurate. Still, the sentiment behind tipping remains the same: a small gesture of gratitude for good service.

In the U.S., we normally tip in restaurants and service-based industries, such as hair and nail salons, and while traveling. But as our society has evolved, tips have seeped more and more into our everyday dealings. Self-service checkout devices are the standard now, and the request for a tip is built in.

The use of technology has changed our transactions and made them very public. You can be at a checkout counter, the movie theater, a self-service car wash, or in a restaurant, and the device present will not only collect your fee but will present a variety of options for tip amounts. Because specific amounts are glaring on the screen or there is a giant "No Tip" option, people feel that societal pressure to tip just to get over with awkward moment. Many individuals will tip even though they are not certain they should. I will answer that question later in this section.

During the COVID-19 pandemic, many Americans went above and beyond with tips because they wanted to do their part to help folks in service-based industries that were shuttered due to lockdowns. But once the lockdowns ended, the request for tips not only seeped into more places, but the "optional" tip amounts were higher than before. So, folks were left with the question of whom to tip, when to tip, and how much to tip. All of the requests for tips have caused a bit of confusion, frustration, and decision fatigue. There's a term that started to circle and people began to refer to the phenomenon as "Tip-flation."

I'm going to take some time to break this whole thing down to you and provide you with some key antidotes to help you navigate tipping. This will allow you to tip (or not tip) with confidence, fairness to others, and sensibility for your own financial well-being.

TIPPING – TIMES WHEN YOU'RE OFF THE HOOK

Before we get into who you should tip and exactly how much you should tip them, I want to ease your mind and share who is not in the tipping category.

There is a whole group of individuals whom you should not tip at all. These are folks who perform within a specific trade, or they are people who earn an actual salary. Here's a list of some of those individuals.

PEOPLE IN EDUCATIONAL OR MEDICAL FIELDS	*Teachers	Doctors	Dentists	Veterinarians*
PEOPLE IN PROFESSIONAL FIELDS	*Life Coaches	Attorneys	Contractors Large Business Owners	Coaches or Camp Counselors*

DON'T TIP PACKAGE DELIVERY PERSONS

Now, these are not individuals who are gig workers who deliver items using app-based technology. I'm referring to people who are employed by companies such as FedEx or UPS. Many of these companies discourage tipping because they do not want to put their drivers at risk by having them carry cash.

DON'T TIP U.S. POSTAL WORKERS

It's actually illegal because these people are government workers. The federal government does not allow it. You may, however, give them a gift valued at twenty dollars or less for one occasion, such as a birthday or holiday.

With these individuals, you're completely off the hook, and it's not proper to tip them in any circumstance.

YOU CAN . . . IF YOU WANT TO

Now, with this next group of individuals, this is where it's totally up to you. In each of these instances, it's up to you to make a determination on whether you want to tip or not. Think back to that old-world meaning: "To Improve Prompt Service." A tip was given when the service was stellar. So, if you had great service and you decide that a tip is warranted, then go right ahead. Otherwise, etiquette would dictate that you're not REQUIRED to tip. Let's look at some scenarios.

You don't have to tip when there's an open bar. Let's say you attend a wedding or some sort of special event, and the bar is hosted by the organizer and the drinks are free. You're not required to leave a tip. Sometimes, you might see a tip jar there. Keep in mind that it is a suggestion, not a requirement. The host has taken care of the gratuity as part of the arrangement. If the bartender goes above, they give great service, or you are drinking quite a bit, then it is acceptable to leave a tip. You can give a dollar or two for each drink.

You don't have to tip when the gratuity is already applied. If you dine at a restaurant and are part of a large party, the establishment will automatically apply the gratuity. Some restaurants have a standard practice where the gratuity is already included. If it is, then there's no need for you to tip.

You don't have to tip for the same service twice. Let's say you get your nails done and you tip the nail technician directly. Then when you get to the counter to pay you may be asked to tip again. It's in this instance where you do not have to tip.

TIPPING IN NAIL AND HAIR SALONS

With nail salons and hair salons, it's a good idea to bring money with you so you can tip the individual technicians. For example, in the nail salon, you'll likely have one person do your nails and another person do your pedicure. In a hair salon, there are often multiple individuals who serve you— from the colorist to the shampooer to the person who styles your hair. The average tip in both nail and beauty salons is 15 to 20 percent. If you have more than one person working on you, it's okay to divide the tip or give each person something individually. A shampooer or assistant might receive $5 to $10 depending on the level of service.

TIPPING WHEN YOU ARE PICKING UP YOUR TAKEOUT FOOD

The tip at the takeout counter of a restaurant is subjective. You're not "required" to leave a tip although it is thoughtful to do so. You can call your order in by phone or app or order directly from the restaurant, pay for your food, say thank you, and walk away. Should you receive great service or you feel as though the restaurant was extra busy and a tip is warranted, you can give one. Anywhere from 5 to 10 percent is a good tip for takeout.

TIPPING AT THE DELI OR BEVERAGE COUNTER

Then there's the dreaded counter service. This is the one that really gets people, and this is where folks are quite confused, so I'm going to clear it up right now once and for all. I am often asked whether one should tip at the counter. The answer is no. You are not "required" to do so. It's not an etiquette thing. Here's how you can apply it to your memory.

> ### THE STAND OR SIT TIPPING RULE
>
> If you are standing and you're purchasing your food or beverage, then you are not "required" to tip. If you are sitting and someone is serving you, then that's when you're required to tip.

In the U.S., servers are not paid an hourly wage, and they earn their living based on tips, but counter workers are earning an hourly wage. There are two things at play here. The employer is offering the workers a perk. That's the tips, but they're putting it on the backs of the consumers. The other is that the more companies that service the devices that swing around and glare at you and are making you feel pressured to tip, the more those organizations make. Again, they're putting it on the backs of the consumers. Bottom line: you are not required to tip at the counter. It is not an etiquette thing. Now, if the service is great, you are a regular customer, and the person remembers your order, it's a big order, they're very friendly that day, or you just have the extra change in your pocket, then, of course, go right ahead and tip.

TIPPING IN RESTAURANTS

Tips in restaurants are usually done on the post-tax amount, but there's nothing wrong with tipping on the pre-tax amount. The average tip in a restaurant is anywhere from 15 to 20 percent. Anything above 20 percent is when you receive that above average or excellent service.

Regardless of how bad the service is or how tight your budget is, always, always leave a tip. It's important to keep in mind that servers do not earn an hourly wage, so your tip is their payment for the service they performed. Albeit bad, you should still compensate them for the work they did.

It's perfectly fine to reflect unsatisfied service with your tip. First, give your server the opportunity to correct the problem and if that does not happen then, you can reiterate your concerns about the poor service to the management. Finally, allow your tip to reflect the service. The bottom rate would be 10 percent. If you don't do this in these steps, your server will not know you were dissatisfied, and they may think you were just mean or cheap.

When using coupons or gift cards, you still tip based on the amount BEFORE the discount. The key here is that you consumed or purchased full-priced food at a discounted rate. The server did not give you discounted work; they still gave you full-service work so they should receive a full-service tip. The gratuity has everything to do with the service. We use the cost of the meal as a guideline to gauge the dollar amount we tip.

If you are at a buffet where you serve yourself, you should leave a tip for the individual who is clearing your table and refilling your drinks. The tip can be anywhere from three to five dollars or more, depending on the number of people in your party and the level of service rendered.

TIPPING DELIVERY SERVICES (FOOD, GROCERIES, HOUSEHOLD GOODS)

When it comes to tipping delivery services, you can follow the tipping guidelines presented by the app you're using in terms of percentage. It is a good practice to tip these individuals, because they are often dealing with things like weather, stairs, or other obstacles just to get to your home. Tipping shows appreciation for their effort.

It is also acceptable to tip after the service has been provided rather than through the app. If you choose to do this, I recommend that you disclose that information as part of your order, so the shopper or delivery person knows that you do intend to tip. That clarity helps set expectations and lets the person know that you fully intend to tip them.

HOW MUCH TO TIP FOR APP-BASED DELIVERIES:

Food Delivery: 15 to 20 percent of the total order is standard. If the weather is bad, your order is large, or the driver had to go up multiple flights of stairs, you can lean closer to 20 percent.

Grocery and Household Goods: These often take more time and effort, so 20 percent is appropriate, with a minimum of $5–10 depending on distance, number of bags, or complexity of the order.

Tipping in Cash After Delivery: Make sure the amount reflects both the effort and time required. Generally, it should never be less than $5, unless it's an unusually small, local order.

HOLIDAY TIPPING HAS EVOLVED

During the holidays, people ask, "Who do I tip? How much do I tip? And how can it get it to them?" Well, I'd like to share the brand-new Tipping Guide for the holidays.

First and foremost, who do you tip? You tip individuals who have helped to make your life easy throughout the year. You have a personal relationship with them, and you're connected to them, and you pay them regularly. Think gardener, pool cleaner, dog walker, housekeeper, babysitter.

Second, what do you tip them? Use what I like to call now, the 20, 30, and 50 Percent Rule. You take the cost of the service you normally pay, and for their holiday gift, you give them a tip based on a percentage.

> ◈ THE 20-30-50 HOLIDAY TIPPING RULE
>
> 20 percent if the service was **Good**
>
> 30 percent if the service was **Great**
>
> 50 percent if the service was **Exceptional**

You tip based on the level of service. The reason why this is a more reasonable approach is because the amount people spend for the services they receive will vary from coast to coast, region to region, city to city, and town to town, so as an etiquette professional, I can't advise you to give one gardener the same amount of tip in Beverly Hills as a gardener in one of our Midwestern states.

Now, for those individuals whom you don't pay at all, maybe it's a doorman or maintenance worker or building superintendent, give those individuals a tip based upon what works best for your budget. Your goal is to show tangible thanks based on what works best for you. Don't be pressured. Feel confident and comfortable. Put that money in an envelope, hand it over, put a nice note in there, and leave it at that. Just make sure that you tip based on what works best for you.

INDIVIDUALS YOU CAN TIP FOR THE HOLIDAYS

♦ *Babysitter or Nanny*

$$ *Caregiver (at a facility)*

♦ *Chauffeur or Driver (if privately hired)*

$$ *Dog Walker or Pet Sitter, Trainer*

$$$ *Doorman or Building Concierge*

♦ *Gardener or Landscaper*

♦ *Hairdresser or Barber*

$$ *Handyman or Regular Contractor*

♦ *Housekeeper or Cleaning Service*

$ *Laundry or Dry Cleaning Delivery Person*

Mail Carrier (limited to $20 value non-cash gifts per USPS guidelines)

$$ *Maintenance Worker or Superintendent*

♦ *Massage Therapist or Esthetician*

♦ *Nail Technician*

$ *Newspaper Delivery Person*

$$ *Parking Garage Attendant*

♦ *Personal Trainer*

♦ *Pool Cleaner*

♦ *Private Nurse or Home Health Aide*

$$$ *Security Guard (in residential buildings)*

$ *Trash or Recycling Collector (check local regulations)*

♦ = **20-30-50 Rule**   Tip a percentage for trusted, year-round service providers.
$ = $10–$30   for occasional or rotating service.
$$ = $30–$75   for steady, moderate service.
$$$ = $75–$100+   for consistent, high-contact service.

For year-round service providers, you may also opt to give the cost of one service, one day, or one week's pay.

TIPPING GUIDELINES ACROSS A VARIETY OF INDUSTRIES

DINING & TRAVEL

Airport Shuttle Driver
$1–2 per bag

Bars
$1 per beer
$1–2 for cocktails
15–20% if you order food

Curbside Check-In
$1–2 per bag

Restaurant
15% for average service
20% or more for superior service

Restaurant Buffet
$3–$5 or more, depending on service and party size

Restaurant Carryout
5–10% if service is exceptional

Restaurant Delivery
10%

Valet
$3–5 tip every one-way ride when staying at a hotel

CARE SERVICES

Babysitter
$5–$10 per child

Barbers
15–20%

Esthetician Services (facials, waxing, etc.)
15–20% depending on quality and complexity

Hair or Nail Salon
15–20% depending on the number of technicians and level of service

Massage or Spa Treatment
15–20% depending on quality and length of session

Pet Groomers
10–20%

Tattoo Artists
15–20%

ERRANDS & EXTRAS

Coat Check
$1–2 per coat

Delivery Apps
10–20%
Minimum $5 for small orders

Furniture or Large-Item Delivery
$5–$10 per person

Grocery Store Clerk
$5

Hotel Bellman
$1–5 per bag

Hotel Housekeeping Service
$2–5 per day depending on the hotel
Tip a bit more for luxury stays or if traveling with children or pets

Movers
$10–20 per mover

Taxi & Rideshares
10–20%

Tour Guides
$5–$10 per person for group tours, more for private

CHAPTER 30

Modern Travel: Preparing, Flying, and Staying with Grace

PREPPING FOR YOUR TRIP

Be prepared. This includes having your ID and passport up to date. Packing weather-specific clothing and bringing snacks for your children and yourself is important. Be especially sure to bring snacks along if you have special dietary needs.

Dress neatly and comfortably. Thirty years ago, folks dressed up to fly. Today, people schlep aboard airplanes looking as if they've just rolled out of bed. Dress nicely so you arrive looking put together. You might even land an upgrade to first class if your appearance matches the part.

If you can't lift it, check it. Test lifting your bag over your head. If you are unable to lift it, then plan to check it or take some items out. You'll avoid paying extra for the bag, and flight attendants are not permitted to lift bags for customers.

AIRPLANE ATTIRE

Yes, in the early days of travel, people would get very dressed up. It was a special occasion to travel. As our world has shifted and changed, and with different classes of travel now in vogue, people today focus on dressing comfortably when traveling.

That's the first thing to look at; however, there are some key things we should take note of when traveling.

Number one, we should always dress in outerwear and not innerwear. Pajamas and things we would wear at home should not be worn when traveling. Look at travel from the perspective of dressing comfortably but also nicely.

Yes, jeans, for example, are acceptable. But we have to remember that airlines still have a dress code. When we go into grocery stores and see a sign on the door that says, "No shoes, no shirt, no service," that's because in our society, we are still expected to present ourselves in a way that does not make other people uncomfortable.

Etiquette is about putting others at ease.

When selecting travel attire, ask yourself, "Can what I'm wearing make anyone else feel uncomfortable?" "Is my low too low?" "Is my high too high?" "Is my tight too tight?"

Although an airplane feels private because there are only a certain number of people there, it is still a public space. We have to think about how we are dressing in public.

Airlines have different classes in the cabin, and those classes have a dress code. If, for example, the main cabin fills up, but there is a seat available in another class, you will not be moved unless you are dressed appropriately.

I share that from the perspective of a former flight attendant for Continental Airlines for ten years. We were instructed not to move people up unless they were dressed appropriately for the first-class cabin. That does not mean you have to wear a three-piece suit, a dress, stockings, and high heels. You just have to dress smartly and chic. If you are wearing leggings and a hoodie? You would likely not be moved up to first class.

There are so many options for attire today. In the past, you were either very dressy or not. Now, we have great athleisure wear that looks stylish and is comfortable for travel.

So, the same way we prepare for travel by making sure we have the appropriate size containers for carry-ons, we should also prepare our travel attire. Select a few items that you wear just for travel and keep them to the side as your go-to travel attire.

You can even say, "This is what I wear when I'm going, and this is what I wear when I'm coming home." That way, your travel outfit is always in good repair, looks great, and is ready to go.

Gate agents will respond to you more positively when you're dressed nicely. It's not a written rule, but it's a known fact in terms of first impressions. People often respond to you based on how you present yourself.

BEHAVIOR AT THE AIRPORT

- Arrive early, anticipate delays. Be prepared to wait in long lines to get through security.

- Follow the rules. Wait your turn when boarding.

- Making special requests gracefully.

BEHAVIOR ON THE PLANE

Power down, please. Turn off your cell phone and portable electronic devices. Just do as you are asked and you'll have a pleasant flight.

Overhead bins are community property. The space just above your seat does not have your name on it. Just place your bag wherever it can fit and sit down. Don't freak out if the flight attendant has to rearrange your bag to accommodate others.

Conversing with your fellow passengers. Greet the person next to you, but keep the conversation brief. If you are a talker, watch for major body language. You'll know if they want you to leave them alone. Communicate politely. If you don't want to engage in further conversation, just excuse yourself to sleep, read, work, or whatever. If you want them to leave you be, just say so. You can say, "Well, it was nice chatting with you. I'm going to rest/read my book/watch the movie now."

Keep it down. Even if you're using headphones, sound can still leak, especially if the volume is too high. If people around you can hear your music, movie, or game, it's too loud. Keep the volume at a level that allows you to enjoy your entertainment without disturbing the passengers nearby. Also, be aware of the content you're watching or playing. If you're sitting next to a child, or even someone who might be uncomfortable, it's a good idea to avoid gruesome, risqué, or overly graphic content. Choose something you'll still enjoy, but that's more appropriate for shared spaces. Being considerate of your surroundings helps everyone have a more pleasant flight.

Be mindful of bodily functions and noises. Watch what you eat before you board. Passing gas is a big NO, NO. If you know that you snore, then bring along breathing strips.

Boarding and seating. Be prepared to move swiftly when boarding the aircraft. If you're carrying both a personal item and a rolling bag, make sure all the handles are untangled and your items are organized. If there's anything you want to keep at your seat with you, take it out before placing your bag in the overhead bin. When you get to your seat, communicate with anyone already sitting nearby to let them know it's your seat. If you're seated by the aisle and the middle or window seats haven't been filled yet, keep your seatbelt unfastened until everyone in your row is seated. Pay attention as people are boarding. Some travelers will speak, while others may simply make a gesture to let you know it's their seat. When that happens, stand up and step back to allow them to enter. When it comes to storing coats or small items, it's best to hold them briefly and prioritize larger bags in the overhead bin. This helps to keep space available for other passengers who may board after you. Then you can always place your coat in the bin at the end of boarding.

If you are sitting in the middle or window seat, it is acceptable to ask the flight attendant to place it there for you instead of asking your whole row to stand.

How to handle seat reclining. Aircrafts are made so that you can recline your seat. You're not required to ask permission from the person behind you.

You can simply lean back. However, my recommendation is to take a quick peek behind you if necessary, especially during food service, to make sure you're not knocking over anyone's food or beverages. Recline your seat slowly. You don't have to slam it back. Just take your time so the person behind you can see that the seat is beginning to move. Now, if you're sitting behind someone and their seat reclines and maybe it spills something or knocks it over, try not to get overly frustrated. Some aircrafts have smaller spaces, and these things can happen. Let the flight attendant know if there's a mess so they can help clean it up. Bottom line: it's absolutely acceptable to recline your seat on an aircraft. Just make sure you're doing so politely and with concern for the person behind you.

Dealing with the armrest. There is always a debate about who gets the armrests when flying. The standard is that the person sitting in the center seat gets both armrests. They are the individual who has the least advantage when it comes to comfort, so either armrest can go to them. When you are flying, simply allow the person in the center seat to have the armrests. If you are in the center, you do not need to ask—those armrests are yours. The armrest can also serve as a form of boundary to maintain privacy. If you don't know the person next to you or you're not traveling together, it's typically better to keep the armrest down. It helps to define your personal space in a polite way. There are some instances when it is acceptable to leave the armrest up. For example, if you are in the aisle seat and another person is in the window seat, and the center seat is empty, then it's fine to put the armrest up so that the two of you can share a little extra space.

Who controls the window shade? The person sitting next to the window controls the window shade. My recommendation is for them to be mindful of when the shade is up and down, based on the time of day and the duration of the flight. Also, just be mindful of the times when people may want to have the shade up.

Let's say, for example, you're landing into an airport where the view is quite popular—it's polite to lift the shade and lean back just a little bit, just in case folks want to take a photo. Pay attention to your seatmates next to you. If you're sitting next to the window and you're taking a photo or video, just glance behind you to see if anyone else is trying to do the same. And if so, just lean back and allow them to. If you're traveling overnight and the cabin is dark, and you get to your destination close to the morning time, pay attention to lifting that shade and letting a bunch of light in—that could be disturbing for people. And if you're sitting in a center or aisle seat and you'd like to look out the window or take a photo, there's nothing wrong with you asking that person to help you.

Freshening up and beauty routines. It's becoming more and more common for people to freshen up or go through parts of their beauty routine while on the plane. My advice is to do things in moderation. If you're doing a full overhaul that takes up a lot of space or might disturb your fellow passengers, it's best to head to the lavatory. Be especially careful with sprays—whether it's perfume, cologne, or facial mist. These can affect the people around you, and not everyone will respond well to strong scents or airborne products. If you're using anything like that, take it into the lavatory. You can absolutely use the lavatory to freshen up but be mindful of how long you're in there. If you know it's going to take some time, especially on a long flight, try to choose a moment when the line isn't long. Just don't overdo it. Be considerate of the other passengers waiting to use the space. Although your seat is your personal space for the duration of the flight, it should not overflow and negatively impact those around you. A little courtesy goes a long way in keeping everyone comfortable.

Asking other passengers to change seats. It is acceptable to ask another passenger to change seats, but it's important to recognize that it is not required.

Sometimes, you may end up sitting separately from your travel companions for one reason or another, and that's okay. If you decide to ask someone to switch, go in prepared to be diplomatic. This is a request—not a demand. Whether you're traveling with small children or simply want to sit with your group, always ask politely. Be mindful of your tone and allow the person to answer honestly. Don't try to make them feel guilty about your situation, and if they say no, you must respect their decision and do what you can to make the best of your travel experience. Also, think about your trade. The switch should ideally be an upgrade or at least a fair exchange for the other person. For example, a middle seat in row 36 might be worth trading for a middle seat in row 13, which is closer to the front of the plane. But if you're offering a downgrade or a less desirable seat, you may need to sit this one out. And if someone says no, don't try to punish them. If you end up seated away from a travel companion, don't reach over another passenger repeatedly or make them feel uncomfortable throughout the flight.

Declining a seat change. Now, if someone asks you to switch seats, remember, you have the right to say no. It might feel awkward or uncomfortable in the moment, but it's okay to prioritize your own comfort. Just be polite in how you decline.

KIND WAYS TO REFUSE A SEAT EXCHANGE.

"Thanks for asking, but I think I'm going to stay in my assigned seat today."

"I'm sorry, I specifically chose this seat, so I'd prefer to keep it."

"I'm not comfortable switching, but I hope you're able t o work something out."

"Unfortunately, I really need the extra space/legroom in this seat, so I'll need to stay here."

These responses are polite and clear, and they set a boundary. The other person might feel bad, disappointed, or frustrated, and that is a natural response. There is nothing you can say or do to change how they feel. So do guilt yourself into taking ownership of their feelings. It will be awkward, but I say embrace the awkwardness, sit back, and do your best to enjoy the rest of your flight.

Bringing food on the plane. First things first: flight attendants do not have a microwave or any heating device onboard to warm up your food. So, whatever you bring, be prepared to eat it as is. Be mindful of the smell of the food you bring. Strong odors can quickly fill the cabin and make the space uncomfortable for others. Try to keep your meal as tidy as possible. We've all seen social media hacks and fancy meal-prep containers, but remember the aircraft is not a food prep kitchen. Don't overdo it. Bring your food, enjoy your meal, but do what you can to minimize mess and not take up too much space while eating or unpacking. Just keep it simple, clean, and considerate.

CHECKING IN AND OUT OF THE HOTEL

The approach to checking out depends on the hotel's standard, which can vary from property to property.

Some people simply leave their key in the room and go. Hotels are aware of this practice, and it is acceptable. If you choose this method, make sure to leave your key in a visible spot such as on the desk or dresser, for example. Dropping the key into a designated box in the lobby is acceptable too.

If you're checking out early, it's thoughtful to consider the housekeeping staff. Leave a tip in the room, remove the "Do Not Disturb" sign, and check out at the front desk, if possible. This makes it clear that your room is available, allowing housekeeping to get a head start. They already have a limited window to clean all the rooms before the next guests arrive, so an early checkout notice helps them manage their workload more efficiently.

When staying somewhere more intimate, like a bed and breakfast, inn, or lodge, the same etiquette applies, except it is conveyed in a more personalized way. Airbnb is different because of its electronic checkout process, but at a bed and breakfast or family-run lodge, it's best to check out face to face. These places often have a more personal atmosphere, and the hosts may want to say goodbye or even offer a parting gift. In that setting, checking out in person is a sign of respect, almost like bidding farewell to a host when leaving someone's home. You don't want to miss out on a farewell moment or a small gift like a candle or a mug!

Overall, your approach to checking out might depend on where you are staying and who's covering the cost. If a client is paying for the room, it is a good practice to check out in person to ensure there are no billing issues. It's courteous and avoids any confusion or unnecessary charges on their end.

Many hotels now offer electronic checkout, especially those with keyless entry. If this option is available, it's perfectly acceptable to use it. It provides a clear record that you have checked out and eliminates the need for a front desk visit. I once stayed at a conference hotel in Las Vegas where the check-in and checkout lines were unbelievably long. Thankfully, they offered an electronic option, which saved me from waiting in line, both coming and going.

Respect Elevator Etiquette. Once you get to the elevator, be respectful of others who are getting off or waiting to get on. Wait for others to enter before selecting your floor. Be polite and wait for others to get on before pushing the button for your floor. If you have suitcases or bags, push them out of the way as best as possible. Don't play with the buttons on the elevator.

Minimize Your Messes. Pick up and wipe down any spilled food or beverages. Place any throwaway items in a wastebasket. Always flush the toilet.

Don't Leave a Wet Mess. Hotel staff should not have to pick up wet towels and washcloths from all over the hotel room. Be courteous and try to keep used towels in one area, such as the bathroom. Before you leave the room for the day, place your dirty towels in a pile on one spot of the bathroom floor.

TRAVELING WITH FRIENDS AND FAMILY

When you're traveling with friends and family, it's important that you remember that people live differently. Some are organized, others are not. Some like a little mess; some prefer very pristine spaces. The one rule you should follow, regardless of how you conduct your normal life, is to clean up after yourself in shared spaces, most especially when you're with a group.

If you're planning the trip, my recommendation is to pair people together who live in the same manner. So, you would put your tidy folks with the tidy folks, and your not-so-tidy ones with the not-so-tidy ones. And if you approach it from this perspective, it will help minimize any conflict and it'll create a more comfortable experience for everyone.

I often say that etiquette is about putting others at ease, and so we definitely don't want to make people feel uneasy when they're sharing a space, whether it's a hotel, a home, or an Airbnb. This is where it's important to just ask and keep communication open. Have conversations about everything from sleeping arrangements to how you're going to share items and daily routines.

One area where conflict typically becomes more prevalent is around timelines. If folks are always waiting for you to show up for breakfast, lunch, or dinner, that can really make it an uncomfortable trip. So, keep in mind that small things can pile up and eventually get on other people's nerves. Respect the group's time, and if you find that you're going to run late, let everybody know. And if that means that you have to allow people to go along without you so that they can still enjoy the trip, then do so.

As you're on the trip, it is good to document the trip itself, but don't let taking photos or videos distract from everyone else's experience. Be mindful of the times when you're capturing the moment. Sometimes it's just important to live in the moment and stay connected. If you go out on an excursion and then come back for lunch later on, you should not sit at the table uploading photos to social media. Instead, my recommendation is that you just leave some time at the end of the day or even the end of your trip before you begin to post on social media.

When you're planning the trip, take note of the demographics and the budget of the people that you've invited. Individuals might have various levels of income, and so you want to find experiences that can meet folks in the middle. Avoid planning any trip that has too many luxury outings, because some folks may have a more modest budget. The important thing to think about in this instance is that everyone should feel included.

If you have to pick up and do some extra cleaning for the betterment of the group, it's best to do so rather than complain. That includes the bathroom, cooking, and television. And, therefore, the weight of responsibility should be shared by everyone. This will help make it a smoother and more enjoyable trip for everyone around.

AIRBNB AND VACATION RENTAL ETIQUETTE

This is a checklist that will help you keep the peace and show respect when you are renting and sharing a space with others.

- ☐ Check in respectfully. Arrive at the agreed-upon time, and if you're running late, communicate. Don't show up early and expect the place to be ready unless you've cleared it in advance.

- ☐ Clean up after yourself during your stay. Even if you're not the tidiest person at home, be mindful that this place does not belong to you and you have to take good care of it.

- ☐ Check with the host's guidelines when it comes to posting pictures or videos. Don't assume everyone wants their vacation or private home online. It only takes a second to review what the standard is for the property you are staying in.

☐ Check out responsibly. Follow the host's checkout instructions. Take out the trash if asked, gather used towels, and leave the space how you found it or even better than you found it.

☐ Take a moment to write in the guest book if the host provides one. This is something that they find valuable in terms of feedback. You don't have to add your private information, like your name, but it is helpful for other guests to learn about your experience at that particular property.

CHAPTER 31

Modern Travel and Leisure Activities

TECHNOLOGY ETIQUETTE WHILE TRAVELING

Technology is completely present in how we travel today, from booking our flights to navigating new cities, and even documenting our experiences while we're on the road. However, just because technology is everywhere, that doesn't mean that we should forget some basic manners surrounding it. Here's a few things that are important to keep in mind.

Don't block walkways or crowd gates while using your phone. It's easy to get caught up in a call or scroll through your phone while standing in line or walking through the airport. But be aware of your surroundings. Don't block busy walkways, boarding areas, or doorways while looking down at your screen.

Respect no-phone zones. If you're in a lounge or a quiet area or even onboard the aircraft during boarding, keep the volume down and keep conversations short.

Put your phone away during announcements and while interacting with gate agents or flight attendants.

Avoid video calls in public areas. FaceTime or doing video meetings in public spaces like airport gates, cafes, or lounges is distracting for those around you. If it's urgent, step aside and take the call in a less crowded spot or switch to audio only. Be courteous when filming or taking photos.

If you're capturing content for social media or taking a quick photo, be aware of who might be in the background. Not everyone wants to be filmed, and it's respectful to give people space and privacy. Charge devices without taking over shared outlets. Use one outlet at a time when charging your phone or laptop, and if you're using a portable power bank or power strip, offer to share it with others nearby. Don't unplug someone else's device to charge your own without asking.

INTERNATIONAL TRAVEL ETIQUETTE

If you're traveling abroad for business, be sure to revisit the section on "Navigating Business in Different Cultures" located in the Business Etiquette chapter. There, I share important insights on greetings, personal space, tipping customs, and cultural expectations across different regions.

For personal or leisure travel, many of those same principles still apply: be respectful, do your research, and adjust your behavior to fit the culture you're visiting. A little awareness goes a long way when you're representing yourself and your country on foreign soil. Here are some key guidelines to follow:

Learn basic greetings and phrases. Even if you don't speak the language, learning how to say "hello," "please," "thank you," and "excuse me" goes a long way.

It shows respect and effort, and people are often more willing to help when you've made a gesture of cultural courtesy.

Dress according to local norms. What's considered casual in your home country might be inappropriate somewhere else. Do a little research to find out if you'll need to cover your shoulders, remove your shoes indoors, or dress more modestly at certain landmarks or places of worship.

Observe local dining customs. From table manners to tipping, eating habits vary widely. In some countries, slurping is a compliment, while in others it's considered rude. Some cultures use utensils differently or not at all. If you're unsure, observe others or ask.

Respect religious and cultural spaces. When visiting temples, churches, or mosques, be mindful of how you enter, how you dress, and where you take photos. Some places have areas where photos are prohibited or where silence is expected. When in doubt, follow the locals' lead.

Use respectful body language. A gesture as simple as a thumbs-up or pointing might have a completely different meaning in another country. Be mindful of your hand gestures, posture, and avoid overly expressive or animated movements unless that's the cultural norm.

Avoid assumptions and stereotypes. Don't treat your trip like a spectacle. Approach other cultures with curiosity, not judgment. Just because something is different doesn't mean it's wrong. Respect the customs, even if they're unfamiliar to you.

Be a mindful tourist. Watch your volume in public places, avoid littering, and don't expect everything to be just like home. Be open to the experience. You're a guest in someone else's country, so travel with grace, humility, and awareness.

TRAINS

- Exercise safety and caution when you are waiting on the platform.

- Wait until others exit before you enter. Step to the side and allow others to exit the train before you step inside.

- Take up space in only one seat. Trains are meant to move a lot of people at a time, so taking up more than one seat can be considered quite rude. If you find that you are on the train for a long ride and there are very few passengers on the train, you may place your belongings on the seat next to you. Keep in mind that if the train has become full, you must remove your belongings to allow someone else to sit down.

- Please do not put your feet or shoes on the seats. The seats on the train are meant for bottoms, not feet or shoes. It's very inconsiderate to place your dirty shoes in a place where someone is meant to sit.

- There is no assigned seating. Riders may sit in any seat that is open. Do your best to stay with your family or in your group. Just know, unlike an airplane, there is no assigned seating for trains. There might be some instances where you are assigned to a certain class or "car" for the train ride. This is not true for subway trains.

- Please use headphones when listening to music or watching videos. It's a good idea to keep yourself occupied, but be mindful of the other passengers around you.

- Use your inside voice. The noise on the train may be louder than normal, which might cause you to want to speak louder. Be mindful of whether you're speaking too loudly. It can be very disruptive to your fellow passengers.

- Be considerate of others (the elderly, people with very small children, or visible disabilities). Offer them your seat if you see the need to do so.

BUSES

LET PASSENGERS EXIT FIRST

When you are on the bus and the doors of the bus open, always allow the passengers who are inside to leave first. Stand to the right or the left of the doors, allowing people to pass by. It's polite to allow parents with strollers or small children, the disabled, and senior citizens to exit the bus first.

ONE SEAT PER PERSON

If you have a backpack or a bag, it's best to hold them on your lap or place them directly underneath the seat you are sitting on. Do not block the aisle. You should only place them in an empty seat next to you if you are on a long ride and they're very few individuals on the bus. If more individuals arrive, you must move your belongings out of the seat to allow someone else to sit there.

SHARE THE SAFETY POLE

Do not lean your body on the pole. This will prevent others from being able to hold on to it. Simply leave enough room for your fellow passengers to hold on.

PREVENT FROM SPREADING GERMS

If you have to cough or sneeze, don't do it in your hand and transfer your germs to the safety pole. Instead, use your elbow or cover your mouth with a tissue.

NOTE THE PRIORITY SEATING SIGNS

On some buses you will find signs for priority seating that is reserved for an individual who is pregnant, disabled, or elderly. You can sit there only if it is unoccupied, but be prepared to give your seat up to the passengers who are designated for this section.

CARPOOL ETIQUETTE

There are so many advantages to carpooling, starting with your wallet, convenience, and the environment. Whether you're behind the wheel or along for the ride, keep these rules of the road in mind to avoid etiquette violations.

1. Be sure your vehicle is properly maintained and insurance is current.

2. Be mindful of your "scent." This includes fragrances and body odor.

3. Settle on reimbursement fees and stick to the agreement.

4. Set your guidelines in advance. (Issues to address: food, drinks, smoking, radio choices, etc.)

5. Don't be late. This goes for drivers and passengers.

6. Don't hold people hostage with pit stops.

7. Stick to established seating preferences to avoid awkwardness.

8. Have a plan B for emergency situations.

9. Avoid talking on your cell phone for long periods of time.

10. Make sure the same rules apply to everyone.

11. Eventually, a carpool becomes a community. It is built on mutual respect, shared routines, and the understanding that riding together benefits everyone.

RENTAL CARS

If you are riding in a rental car, be extra careful of spills from food and beverages. It's important to keep the car neat and tidy, just as you would your own.

You are responsible for any damage to the vehicle. Do not destroy anything inside the car. This includes the seats that you sit on and the backs of the seats in front of you. Take note of anything you find broken or out of place even if it is after you have completed the inspection and taken possession of the vehicle.

RULES OF VALET PARKING

Valet parking is a luxury that many people take for granted. While it seems that everyone wants excellent service, few are willing to give extra dollars for superb labor. Here are five rules for valet parking.

1. Remove all distractions. Turn off the navigation, put your cell phone in your pocket or purse, and focus on the attendant. Removing all distractions will ensure that directions are followed and the process goes smoothly.

2. Look the attendant in the eye. They are not just someone who fetches your vehicle. They are people. They deserve your undivided attention and respect. Make eye contact with the attendant and address them by name when feasible.

3. Present a clean car. Your truck or car may be like your second home, but the valet shouldn't know that. Put everything in the back/trunk and present the attendant with a clean car so that he doesn't have to worry about damaging your valuables.

4. Tip according to the level of service. It is generally a good idea to give the attendant a tip just for parking your car. After all, they are making your life easier by taking care of your vehicle. An attendant who goes above the call of duty by going back to your car to retrieve something that you left should get more in the way of tipping. In fact, anything beyond parking your car deserves more money.

5. Learn the ways of gratuity. Some restaurants and hotels allow for credit card tipping, while others only let their valet attendants receive gratuity in cash. It is essential that you call in advance to ensure that you are prepared to tip your server.

MUSEUMS AND NATIONAL MONUMENTS

When visiting museums or national landmarks, remember that these spaces are meant to be respected, preserved, and enjoyed by everyone. Your behavior should reflect an appreciation for both the environment and the experience of others.

GENERAL CONDUCT:

- Walk, don't run. This is for your safety and the safety of the exhibits.

- Avoid leaning on walls, display cases, or any structural surfaces.

- Keep your voice low and avoid disruptive conversations. Treat the space as one of reflection and learning.

- Be respectful and courteous to museum staff and tour guides.

BAGS AND BELONGINGS:

- Avoid bringing backpacks or large bags. Many institutions require you to check them or may not allow them in galleries.

- Don't bring food or drink into exhibition areas.

PHONES AND PHOTOGRAPHY:

- Silence your phone and avoid making calls during tours or while walking through exhibits.

- Photography is often permitted, but always check the posted rules. Refrain from using flash, and leave selfie sticks at home, they're often prohibited to protect the art.

ARTWORK AND DISPLAYS:

- Do not touch the art or lean on pedestals, even if it seems like a stable surface.

- Never touch glass cases or mounted displays unless explicitly allowed.

- Follow signage closely. If it says "Do Not Touch," respect that instruction.

MOVING THROUGH THE SPACE:

- Stay with your group if you're on a guided tour, including through galleries, gift shops, and cafés.

- Be aware of your surroundings when using elevators or escalators. Step aside promptly to keep foot traffic flowing.

CHAPTER 32

Houseguest Etiquette

RESPECT THE WISHES OF THE HOST

When you're invited to someone's home for dinner or a party and they tell you not to bring anything, I advise you against bringing something anyway. The core value of etiquette is respect, and you should respect their request. Hosts make that declaration for a number of reasons. Maybe they've got everything and can't take another widget or trinket in the house. Maybe they don't want to pair your wine with their meal. They might simply be in more of a giving mood. If someone asks you not to bring anything, resist the urge. They'll be more grateful that you listened to what they said than if you brought over more "stuff."

BRING SERVING UTENSILS

When you're invited to a potluck, an extra special thing to do is to bring serving utensils along with your dish. This way, the host can easily serve the food. A lot of times, the host may already have utensils, but the thoughtful thing to do is to make things easy for them. Bring the utensils, leave them there, as a hostess gift. If they are disposable let the host toss them out when they're ready.

LEFTOVERS

If you are asked to bring a dish for a potluck dinner and there are leftovers, leave them there. Do not take the leftovers home with you. The purpose of bringing a dish is to contribute, and you should honor that contribution. If you really enjoyed the dish you made, set some aside for yourself at home before you go. But whatever you take to the host's house should stay there. Another thoughtful gesture is to bring your dish in a platter or bowl that can be left with the host as a gift. It's a small act of kindness that leaves a lasting impression.

OFFERING TO HELP CLEAN UP

If you're invited to someone's home for dinner or a party and you offer to help set up or clean up, but the host declines, simply respect for their request. Not everyone wants guests in their space. Most hosts have their own way of doing things and may prefer to enjoy their guests rather than be separated from them by cleaning up. If they say no, honor their wishes and let them handle it their way. It's a simple way to show courtesy and respect for their hospitality.

MAKE SURE YOUR CHILDREN MIND THEIR MANNERS

If your children are visiting someone's home with you, ensure they follow house rules, respect personal belongings, and maintain a reasonable noise level, especially if the host has no children.

DON'T BRING TOO MUCH LUGGAGE

Make sure your luggage is manageable and doesn't clutter shared spaces, like hallways or living areas.

SETTING A CLEAR DEPARTURE DATE IN ADVANCE

Did you and your host agree you'd leave on Sunday evening? As a great houseguest, you do just that. Ask just about any host, and they'll tell you that a guest overstaying their welcome is one of their biggest pet peeves. If a guest has pushed the boundary, the host is right to speak up. It's not always the easiest conversation to have, but it is absolutely necessary for the host to ask the guest to leave. Your tone should be polite, yet firm. Say something along the lines of, "Hey [friend], I'm going to have to ask you to end your stay as of tomorrow morning." Follow this up with some nicety that rings true to your relationship. Don't buckle in and give them a way out—be very direct. Avoid open-ended stays. When making arrangements, establish start and end dates so your host knows exactly when to expect you.

If your departure is flexible (e.g., due to a medical procedure or changing plans), communicate that early: "I'm planning to leave on [date], but there's a small chance I may need to stay an extra day or two. I'll keep you updated."

You leave as planned. Do not overstay your welcome.

Stick to the agreed duration of your stay, and if there's a need to extend, ask well in advance and be willing to accommodate any inconvenience this may cause.

BRING A GIFT OR TREAT TO YOUR HOST

Personalized gifts that reflect your host's preferences, such as a favorite bottle of wine or a book they've mentioned, can add a thoughtful touch. As a guest, you should either bring a gift, send a thank-you gift afterward, or contribute during your stay.

Options include:

1. A thank-you gift after your stay – A handwritten note with a thoughtful present.

2. A small gift upon arrival – A bottle of wine, flowers, or a personalized item.

3. Hosting an experience during your visit – Taking the family out to dinner, treating them to a meal, or organizing a fun activity.

A great way to show gratitude is to provide something of joy for your hosts.

The guest should always extend thanks to the host for staying at their home, and they should give a gift. Some classic gifts include flowers or a food basket. Or you can give money that goes towards housekeeping or the replenishment of supplies.

ADAPT TO THE HOUSEHOLD'S ROUTINE

When staying in someone's home, observe the flow of the house and adjust accordingly. If your hosts are early risers, try not to sleep in excessively late. If they dress for breakfast, consider doing the same. Your goal is to be in sync with the household's rhythm so that your presence doesn't create discomfort. Your host is an early riser and serves breakfast at sunrise. How does this affect your mornings?

DON'T BRING A STRANGER INTO THE HOME

Do not use someone's home as a dating crash pad. This includes bringing a one-night stand or a Tinder date back to your host's house. If you are staying with friends or family, respect their space and get permission before bringing guests over.

SHARING YOUR SCHEDULE WITH THE HOST

You do not need to report your every move, but it's polite to let your host know your general plans. If you're visiting them specifically and planning to spend time together, inform them of any outside plans you may have. If you're staying there for convenience (e.g., a work trip), a simple "I'll be in and out throughout the day" is fine. You come prepared with an itinerary. Some guests figure that since the host lives there, they'll know all the good stuff, the best parks, museums, and restaurants. And while that is likely true—and why it's absolutely okay to ask for—don't treat them like your personal tour guide.

RESPECTING THE HOST'S PRIVACY

Be mindful of privacy and social media when visiting someone's home. It may be tempting to snap a photo or record a video, especially if the space is beautiful or unique, but always ask for permission before doing so. Never post images or videos that show the inside or outside of someone's home without their consent. Be especially careful not to reveal expensive artwork, personal belongings, or private areas, even unintentionally. Respecting someone's home means respecting their privacy, both in person and online.

Be respectful of their personal belongings, and do not go through their cabinets or medicine drawers.

If they wanted you to know their medical history, they'd tell you. Perusing through their medicine cabinets and opening each and every drawer? That's not just bad houseguest behavior—that's simply intrusive, not to mention disrespectful. The very best houseguests know to respect the privacy of the person who is so graciously hosting them.

DON'T TAKE OVER COMMON AREAS

When you're staying in someone else's home, it's important to keep your belongings organized and out of the way. Don't let your suitcase explode all over the living room or your toiletries take over the bathroom counter. Shared spaces like the kitchen, bathroom, or living room should still feel like their home, not your temporary one. Keep your things in your designated area and clean up after yourself throughout your stay. You're a guest, and part of being a gracious guest is making sure your presence doesn't overwhelm the space. The goal is to blend in and not take over.

TOILET ETIQUETTE

Toilet etiquette counts when you're a guest in someone's home. If you need to move your bowels, remember that we are all human, so don't be too embarrassed. The important factor is to know that it is your responsibility to leave the space as fresh and clean as possible.

If you find that the bathroom spray alone isn't enough to address the situation, here's an effective solution. Look for a toilet cleaner placed nearby or in a cabinet. If you see it, use it. Simply swish it around the bowl and flush thoroughly.

If no toilet cleaner is available, use this simple hack: grab a bit of liquid soap. After flushing once or twice, lift the toilet lid, add a few squirts of soap into the water, and swish it around using the toilet brush. Let it sit for a few moments, then flush again. Taking these extra steps shows care and respect for your host's home and ensures you leave the bathroom as pleasant as you found it.

CLEAN UP AFTER YOURSELF

Don't literally make yourself at home. Take responsibility for cleaning any areas you use, including bathroom and kitchen, and offer to help with household chores as a sign of respect. You clean up in each room you touch.

From pools of water on the bathroom floor to wet towels left on the bed (and, not to mention, dirty dishes on the kitchen table—not even in the sink), making messes and leaving them for your host is one of the biggest houseguest offenses. The ultimate houseguest cleans up any mess they create and may even help their host with general tidying up throughout their stay.

Leave your pets at home. Confirm with your host in advance if pets are allowed, and if they are, ensure your pet is well-behaved and doesn't create extra work for the host.

DON'T EAT YOUR HOST OUT OF HOUSE AND HOME

Be conscious of food consumption. If you're staying for more than a few days, offer to cook a meal or cover some grocery expenses. Be mindful of the food you consume. If you're eating their groceries, contribute by restocking or buying a meal.

KEEP YOUR OPINIONS TO YOURSELF

When you're a guest in someone's home, it's not the time to critique or offer unsolicited advice. This also applies to commenting on home décor, lifestyle choices, or parenting styles. Keep conversations light and positive. Focus on making your host feel appreciated and at ease.

RESPECT THE MORAL VALUES OF YOUR HOST

Whether it's regarding diet, religious practices, or daily routines, respecting your host's household values fosters a better relationship. Even if their lifestyle is different from your own, honor their choices while you're in their space. You don't have to agree, but you do have to be courteous.

DON'T ABUSE THE PHONE, INTERNET, OR ANY OTHER PRIVILEGES

Limit your use of household resources, such as long showers or streaming services, especially if your host is paying for them. You also can't expect the host to play chauffeur; ask your host about easy ways to get around town.

FIND YOUR OWN TRANSPORTATION

As a great houseguest, you know that your host isn't a transportation service. You take public transportation (if it's available), walk if your destination is close enough, or call an Uber or Lyft. Simply put, you never put strain on your loved one by making them your chauffeur. A great guest does their own research first and comes prepared with a plan.

STRIPPING THE BED BEFORE YOU LEAVE

Make the bed neatly before you leave. Not all hosts want you to strip the bed. Some prefer to handle the linens themselves, especially if they have a housekeeper or specific laundering routines. Instead, check with your host if they prefer you to strip the bed or leave it as is.

ALWAYS SEND A THANK-YOU NOTE AFTER YOUR VISIT

Handwritten notes are always appreciated, but even a personalized email or text works. Be specific in your gratitude, mentioning things that made the stay special. If you want to go the extra mile, send a gift like flowers or a food basket. Or you can give money that goes towards housekeeping or the replenishment of supplies.

CHAPTER 33

Hosting Etiquette

GREETING GUESTS AT THE DOOR

When you're hosting, make it a point to greet your guests at the door. It doesn't have to be grand, but it should be warm and prompt. It's also a good idea to have something waiting for them, maybe a signature welcome drink and some appetizers already out. Try not to be in the kitchen when guests arrive. I know that's not always easy, but if you are still working on something, then designate someone else to greet your guests at the door.

MUSIC, LIGHTING, AND AMBIENCE

If you're playing music, keep it low enough for people to talk without having to raise their voices. Match the vibe of your gathering with the right playlist, perhaps something that creates atmosphere without taking over.

Also, pay attention to your lighting. For cocktail-style gatherings, go for low lights, subtle fragrance, and great music. For the holidays, bring in brighter lighting and a more festive, cheery feel. Let your lighting set the mood.

BEING MINDFUL OF SCENTS

Not everyone experiences fragrance the same way. A scent that you love might be too strong or irritating to someone else. That said, I recommend placing a lightly scented candle near the entrance of your home. It's a beautiful way to set the tone. The scent can change depending on the season. Here are a few suggestions:

SPRING	*lavender, citrus blossom, jasmine*
SUMMER	*coconut & lime, sea salt, gardenia*
FALL	*pumpkin spice, apple cinnamon, amber & fig*
WINTER	*pine, vanilla, clove, peppermint*

MAKE ROOM FOR GUESTS COATS AND BAGS

Set aside either a room or extra closet in your home for these additions. Keeping items in one specific place guarantees their safety and eliminates chaos. The worst thing to do is wait until guests arrive and pile their belongings on the back of your sofa.

HAVE ENOUGH SEATING FOR YOUR GUESTS

One thing you should definitely have for your guests is plenty of seating. Get a good headcount or estimate of your guests. Don't worry about everything having to match, but bring seating from anywhere you can. And don't be afraid to rent some chairs if you need to as well. It's better to have more than enough seating than not having any at all.

STOCKING THE GUEST BATHROOM

If you're having people over, make sure the bathroom is fully stocked. That includes fresh hand towels, bathroom spray, soap, and lotion. It's also thoughtful to have a small first aid kit accessible in case of any mishaps.

HOSTING A POTLUCK AT HOME

You're hosting a potluck at your home. The best approach is to figure out your overall theme of your meal. Get a list going of what is needed by putting it into categories and then communicating with those who are going to attend so that things stay organized. You can have one approach where everybody contributes in several ways, or you can have another approach where you do all of the main dishes and then you make assignments for side dishes. Keep in mind everything else you'd like to include. That could be everything from cutlery to beverages.

It's acceptable to ask people to contribute money to a shared potluck—if that's the plan. For example, let's say you're hosting a big watch party for a major sporting event and, instead of cooking, you've all decided to order from a favorite restaurant. In that case, everyone pitching in is totally fine.

But you don't want it to turn into a situation where people feel like they're paying an actual fee just to eat at your house. So be careful how you organize it, how you word it, and what your intention is behind it.

HOW TO SET A BUFFET

When setting up a buffet at home, start with the plates, followed by the meats, then the starches, and finally the vegetables. Place the cutlery and napkins at the end of the buffet. This setup allows guests to have their hands free to serve themselves as they move down the line. Following this order will help you create the perfect buffet experience for your guests.

SETTING EXPECTATIONS FOR CHILDREN

If children will be attending your gathering, plan ahead. You can create a play zone with activities like arts and crafts or things they can build. For teenagers, you might give them a fun assignment. You can have them use their phones to go around and interview family members or guests, then create a little video or Reel that everyone can enjoy later.

WHEN A GUEST BRINGS A BOTTLE OF WINE

If a house guest brings a bottle of wine, you do not have to open it automatically. It is a gift, and a gift should be enjoyed at your leisure, so you can just put it away. And, of course, graciously say thank you.

HANDLING AN UNEXPECTED GUEST

If an unexpected guest arrives at your home, etiquette is about putting others at ease. The best thing for you to do is welcome that guest, set out another plate, another glass, another set of food, and graciously make that person feel warm, welcome, and invited. Don't say anything to the individual who may have brought the extra guest, at least not at that time. If it causes a big strain, you can always address it later, after the event is over, but do so privately. But never make a person feel as though they are not welcome.

WHEN A GUEST BRINGS A PET WITHOUT ASKING

If your house guest unexpectedly arrives with their pet, it is acceptable for you to set your own personal boundaries. So, give them the opportunity to make a choice. You might state that you have a certain area that you prefer for their pet to stay in. If it's not acceptable to them, then you can give them some recommendations for a local kennel. But do not feel compelled to overturn your house. You'll be miserable the entire time they're there, and not setting your boundaries can cause resentment.

ACCOMMODATING A GUEST'S NEW DIETARY PREFERENCE

If you have invited folks to dinner and it is already prepared and your dinner guest announces that they are now vegan or vegetarian or something to that effect and you were not prepared, do what you can to maybe add an additional side dish in order to best accommodate them and then point it out. There is no need for you to do a whole overhaul of your meal, but don't make the guest feel bad about their change. Never put people on the spot because you never know why they've made particular changes.

HOW TO ENCOURAGE PARTY GUESTS TO LEAVE

There are three steps you can take to get guests to leave when the party is over.

Step One

If there's music or television blaring, first turn it down. This will create a little bit of an awkward but necessary silence.

Step Two

If the lights are dim, turn them up so that people can start to feel as though things are coming to an end. You can also begin to put bags and outerwear, such as coats and scarves, near the door.

Step Three

If people do not get the hint that it's time to leave, tell them. There's nothing wrong with saying something like, "Well, thank you all so much for coming. I'm going to go ahead and call it a night."

PARTING GIFTS FOR GUESTS

It's always a nice touch to send your guests away with a small gift. For holiday gatherings, maybe it's a mug with hot cocoa or a bag of cookies. For something like Easter, it might be a small loaf of sweet bread. The gift doesn't have to be fancy; it just needs to feel thoughtful and reflect the occasion.

GUEST FOLLOW-UP ETIQUETTE

A handwritten thank-you note is always appreciated, especially if someone went out of their way to help make the gathering a success. That said, it is absolutely acceptable to send a follow-up text message. A quick message to say, "Thank you so much for coming," goes a long way.

HOSTING OVERNIGHT GUESTS

PREPARING THE SLEEPING AREA

Whether it's a dedicated guest room or a pull-out couch, make the sleeping area feel intentional. Have clean sheets, extra blankets, and a few comforts waiting. A welcome basket is a thoughtful touch. It could include items like cozy socks, a puzzle book, lotions, or a tote bag they can take with them. Include a couple of water bottles in the room as well. Just be mindful of any full-size items if they're flying. Stick to travel sizes when possible. If you don't have a dresser, consider using a hanging closet organizer to give them a place to store their things. Don't forget to include hangers and make a little space in the closet if possible.

RESPECT THEIR PRIVACY

Give your guests space. Don't walk into the room they're staying in without knocking. If they're having a personal conversation, even though they're in your home, just walk away and allow them the moment.

PREPARE WITH FOOD

Ask about their dietary preferences before they arrive. Even if their preferences are different from yours, have a few options available. Also, stock the house with snacks, especially if you're not a snacker yourself and place a few bottles of water in the guest room for convenience.

WI-FI AND ENTERTAINMENT

Print out the Wi-Fi name and password and place it somewhere visible or include it in the welcome basket. Offer some entertainment options, too. That might mean giving them access to guest accounts on your streaming services, having books or board games available, or curating a fun music playlist they can enjoy.

WHEN AN OVERNIGHT GUEST LEAVES THEIR ROOM MESSY

If you have an overnight guest and they don't make their bed or keep their room tidy, just mind your business. Close the door. Allow them to have their space. Just keep in mind it's not forever.

WHEN A GUEST NEEDS TRANSPORTATION

If your houseguest wants to take day trips but didn't rent a car and they're hinting for a ride, it's okay to say no. If it doesn't fit your schedule, kindly let them know and suggest alternatives like Uber or Lyft. If needed, you can help them schedule a ride in advance or recommend a car rental.

WHEN A GUEST TAKES LONG SHOWERS

If you have a houseguest that's been taking long showers and using up the hot water, it is absolutely acceptable for you to bring it to their attention. Just do so when they're not in the shower and let them know why. Maybe your plumbing is a little older, your water tank is low, but give them the reasoning behind it so they understand.

WHEN A GUEST HOGS THE TV

If you have a houseguest that likes a particular thing on television and they tend to be hogging it up, do what you can to allow them to enjoy their time that they're there and find another alternative for yourself or maybe just hang out with them. You might just learn something new. If it's something you don't enjoy, then figure out something else that you can do. Maybe journal, read a book, enjoy yourself.

BE A GRACIOUS HOST UNTIL THE END

When it's time for your guests to leave, be helpful. Assist with their bags and gathering their things. Your goodbye is one last chance to show care and sincerity.

PARTY PLANNING COUNTDOWN

Hosting a party at home can be a joyful experience, but it does take some planning. This countdown is designed to walk you through the process step by step so you can stay organized, feel confident, and actually enjoy your own gathering. Whether you're hosting something casual or more formal, having a plan in place will help everything flow more smoothly. Use this as a guide to help you pace yourself and prepare with ease.

FOUR WEEKS OR MORE IN ADVANCE

- ☐ Set your budget

- ☐ Determine the theme and size of your party

- ☐ Decide which part or area of your home you will entertain in

- ☐ Finalize the party date

- ☐ Send save-the-date cards or emails (up to three months in advance if hosting out-of-town guests)

- ☐ Create your invitation list

- ☐ Send your invitations

- ☐ Plan the menu

- ☐ Assemble recipes or book a caterer

- ☐ Arrange for any additional help you might need

- ☐ Reserve rental equipment such as tables, chairs, etc.

THREE WEEKS OR MORE IN ADVANCE

☐ Purchase décor and supplies

☐ Choose parting gifts for guests

☐ Take inventory of cookware, serving dishes, and utensils

☐ Purchase any needed cookware, serving dishes, and utensils

☐ Purchase bathroom or powder room amenities

☐ Call guests to confirm they received their invitation

TWO WEEKS IN ADVANCE

☐ Clean any china, silverware, and crystal you will be using

☐ Launder and iron tablecloths and linen napkins

☐ Do a first round of grocery shopping

☐ Prepare any dishes that can be frozen

ONE WEEK IN ADVANCE

☐ Clean the house thoroughly

☐ Discuss menu details with the caterer (if using one)

☐ Call guests who have not RSVP'd

- [ ] Set the stage by moving large furniture or chairs into place

- [ ] Notify neighbors—confirm parking, foot traffic, and noise expectations

THREE DAYS IN ADVANCE

- [ ] Stage your home

- [ ] Remove any personal items you don't want guests to see

- [ ] Finish grocery shopping

- [ ] Make a detailed cooking schedule for your planned dishes

- [ ] Set up a clean-up station area, bin, or basket

- [ ] Begin to decorate

ONE DAY IN ADVANCE

- [ ] Buy and arrange flowers

- [ ] Pre-set the table

- [ ] Set up the buffet (if having one)

- [ ] Complete the majority of your cooking

- [ ] Place guest amenities in the bathroom or powder room

- [ ] Complete any food prep (e.g., marinating, dicing, cutting)

- [ ] Finalize your design and décor

DAY OF THE PARTY

- [ ] Finish the final cooking and food preparation

- [ ] Chill beverage glasses

- [ ] Set your final table and place settings

- [ ] Set food out for display

- [ ] Turn on music

- [ ] Be ready to greet your guests as they arrive

PART SEVEN

Relationships, Celebrations, and Life Events

HONORING LIFE'S MILESTONES

WITH GRACE AND JOY

The true measure of etiquette is not in the party, but in the way we care for people through life's milestones.

- ELAINE SWANN -

CHAPTER 34

Family and Friendships

The true measure of etiquette is not in the party, but in the way we care for people through life's milestones. Our lives are marked by moments: birthdays, graduations, weddings, and even goodbyes. These events are opportunities for us to show up for the people we love with presence, purpose, and poise. In this final section, you'll find guidance for handling everything from dating etiquette to hosting for the holidays, entertaining in your home, and taking in the joy of a wedding. This is not just about doing things the right way; it's about honoring other people in the process. And that, more than anything at all, is the heart of all things etiquette.

HOW TO OFFER A SINCERE APOLOGY

A good apology is short, sincere, and free of excuses. Start by owning your actions and acknowledging the impact. Your apology might sound like this: "I'm sorry for what I said. I now realize it was hurtful." Avoid saying, "I'm sorry you took it that way, but that's not what I meant."

The first takes ownership and validates the other person's feelings. The second deflects responsibility and focuses on intent instead of impact.

HOW TO GRACEFULLY ACCEPT AN APOLOGY

When someone comes to you to apologize, let them speak. Do not interrupt. Let them get it all out, admit what they did, and give the apology.

When they're done, say, "Thank you for the apology. I appreciate it." And that's it. Don't say anything else. Too often we feel awkward and say, "It's okay." But it's not okay. If they feel the need to apologize, then it wasn't okay to them. So let them do it. Be gracious. Be graceful. Be quiet. Just say thank you for the apology.

FOUR STEPS TO TAKING RESPONSIBILITY FOR MISTAKES

When you find you've made a mistake, don't try to hide it or shift the blame.

> ◇ HERE'S HOW TO HANDLE MISTAKES WITH GRACE
>
> 1. **Own It.** Acknowledge what happened without excuses.
>
> 2. **Apologize.** Say, "I'm sorry" and what you did, briefly, without overexplaining.
>
> 3. **Fix It.** Take steps to make it right.
>
> 4. **Move On.** Don't keep repeating the mistake. Let it go and focus forward.

HOW TO GRACEFULLY SHUT DOWN SOMEONE WHO GOSSIPS, AND WHY IT'S IMPORTANT

Beware of people who gossip about others to you, because they just might be gossiping about you. Proverbs 11:13 says, "A gossip betrays a confidence, but a trustworthy person keeps a secret." So, when someone comes to you and says, "Girl, don't tell nobody I said this, but here's what so-and-so is doing . . ." They are breaking a confidence. And you have to ask yourself, "What makes you so special that they wouldn't do the same thing to you?"

When someone brings gossip your way, stop them in their tracks. You can say, "You know what? She's or he's not here to talk about themselves or to defend themselves, so I just don't want to hear anybody else's business." Stop letting people bring you mess, because chances are, they might be taking your mess to somebody else too.

DON'T GIVE PEOPLE PERMISSION TO INSULT YOU

When someone says, "Can I ask you a question that's a little personal?" it's often a setup for something inappropriate or rude. Saying "okay" gives them permission to cross a line. Here's how to protect yourself:

1. **Pause.** Don't answer right away. Let them reveal their intent first.

2. **Use body language and words:**

   - Body language: Raise your hand slightly in a stop gesture.

- Words: Say, "Hold on. You can ask, and then I'll decide if I want to answer."

3. **Let them ask.** If you're comfortable, answer. If not, say, "You're right. That's too personal, and I'd rather not answer."

4. **Shift.** Change the subject and steer the conversation in a different direction.

HOW TO POLITELY SHUT DOWN MESS AND PROTECT YOUR PEACE AMONG FRIENDS

Here's how to shut down mess, protect your peace, and stop people from bringing drama to you. The next time one of your friends comes and tells you that someone else said something about you, here's what to do:

First, ask one of these two questions:

"So, what did you say when she said that about me?"

or

"I wonder what made her feel so comfortable to say something about me to you?"

Then, follow up with this directive:

"You know what? If this person ever says anything about me again, I don't want you to bring it back to me. I don't want to hear it. I don't want to know about it. I don't want to know anything. Keep it to yourself."

What will happen is that person will no longer feel welcome to bring you a bunch of stuff. They may even fall away and end up on the outside of your inner circle—which is probably where they need to be anyway.

HOW TO DEAL WITH A FRIEND WHO ALWAYS HAS SOMETHING NEGATIVE TO SAY

You have a girlfriend who is a negative Nancy. (Sorry to all the Nancys out there!) Here's how to handle it:

When this person always has something negative to say, especially when good things are happening, you need to call them on the carpet.

Simply say:

"That's not nice. Don't say that. Listen, if something good happens to me, I would prefer for people to either say nothing at all or just wish me well. I'm sure that's the same thing you would want in that instance as well."

Don't let a person come into your space and keep saying negative things about people. Let them know you will not allow it.

HOW TO POLITELY DEAL WITH A FRIEND CANCELING ON YOU AT THE LAST MINUTE

You just got all dolled up, ready to hang out with your girlfriend, and she cancels on you. How do you politely handle this? Bottom line: extend a little bit of grace. You never know what's happening with that person. When they tell you they can't make it, simply say:

"Okay, I hope all is well."

You can always follow up later to find out what the details were if you need to.

Be sure you don't go into a whole explanation about how long it took you to get ready, how last minute it was, or how horrible it is for you, because you never know what the other person is going through.

Just extend a little bit of grace.

HANDLING AWKWARD COMMENTS FROM CHILDREN

Before visiting family or friends, talk to your children about differences in lifestyle and how we don't want to say things that could make others feel bad. One of our core etiquette values is consideration—making sure we're not doing or saying anything that hurts someone's feelings. Have a conversation in advance about what they may see and how to respond. If they have a question about something different from what they're used to, teach them to wait and ask you privately, rather than commenting out loud in front of others.

TEACHING CHILDREN TO SPEAK TO ADULTS RESPECTFULLY

Things have most certainly changed today as it pertains to children speaking up, and it's important that we teach them how to do so with both confidence and respect. One of the key lessons we teach at the Swann School of Protocol is that it is acceptable for children to interrupt an adult, but they must do it politely.

When a child needs to interrupt, teach them to start by saying, "Excuse me." But don't allow them to say "Excuse me" and immediately start talking as though it's a magic word. Instead, they should say, "Excuse me," then wait until they are acknowledged before they begin speaking.

Encouraging children to do this helps them develop the skills they will need to interact successfully in the adult world. When they practice patience and awareness in conversations now, they will carry those habits into adulthood.

Beyond interrupting, it is important to teach children that they can and should share their thoughts, feelings, and ideas. They should be encouraged to be curious, ask questions, and even challenge things they don't understand—but always with respect.

Curiosity is a vital skill that will serve them well as they grow, but it must be paired with good manners.

Teach them to ask questions in a way that invites conversation rather than confrontation. We want to raise children who engage, not argue.

By guiding them in these small but meaningful ways, we help them develop the social skills that will allow them to communicate with confidence, build strong relationships, and navigate life with both kindness and self-assurance.

SIBLINGS AND BIRTHDAY PARTIES

If you receive a birthday party invitation and you're wondering whether your other children can attend, always check with the host first. Don't just assume it's okay to bring siblings along. It's important to respect the host's plans. They've likely accounted for everything from food to space to party favors.

Once you make your inquiry, honor their final answer. If they say no, be prepared to either make other arrangements for your other children or decline the invitation altogether. It's perfectly fine to ask. Just make sure you don't bring siblings along uninvited.

DISCUSSING ESTATE PLANNING AND FINANCIAL SUPPORT FOR AGING PARENTS

We are in an era where many of us are caring for our own children while also becoming more involved with our aging parents. Conversations about estate planning and financial support should never be sprung on siblings or family members. Instead, plan in advance. If you have a family group text, bring up the topic and ask when a good time would be for everyone to discuss it.

Sometimes, we want to have these conversations when everyone is face to face, but that may not be the best time for all involved. A sibling with small children may be distracted and unable to engage in a deep conversation. Just because they are physically present, that doesn't mean they are mentally prepared. To be considerate, send a message in advance and get everyone's buy-in. That way, people can set aside time, both physically and mentally, for the discussion.

HOW TO APPROACH THE CONVERSATION:

1. **Set Expectations** - Let everyone know what the conversation will cover, such as estate planning, healthcare directives, or shared financial responsibilities. This helps avoid surprises.

2. **Choose a Calm Environment** - Avoid bringing it up at family gatherings or during holidays. Instead, schedule a separate time when everyone can focus without distractions.

3. **Stick to Facts, Not Emotions** - Stay focused on practical matters. Avoid blaming or past grievances. Use phrases like, "Here's what I've learned," or "Let's figure out a plan that works for everyone."

4. **Follow Up in Writing** - After the conversation, send a follow-up note summarizing key points and any next steps. This keeps everyone aligned and prevents miscommunication.

CHAPTER 35

Relationships and Dating

ONLINE DATING ETIQUETTE

One thing about internet dating that we have to recognize is that this is an actual forum for you to reach out to a person and let them know you're interested in them. You should, therefore, utilize the options that the platform has to offer to initially connect with someone.

GHOSTING AND BREADCRUMBING EXPLAINED

Ghosting is when someone you've been talking to or dating suddenly cuts off all communication without warning. One day everything seems fine, and the next they're gone. No message, no explanation, just silence.

Breadcrumbing is when someone gives you just enough attention to keep you interested but never actually follows through. They'll like your posts, send a flirty message here and there, maybe even say they want to make plans—but those plans never happen. It's a way of keeping you "on the hook" without committing.

HOW TO HANDLE GHOSTING WITH GRACE

When someone ghosts you, don't go chasing them down. Don't double-text. Don't beg for clarity. As difficult as it may feel in the moment, let their silence be your answer. Ghosting says more about them than it does about you.

Tell yourself, "Thank you for revealing your communication style early." Then move on with grace. Anyone who can't even offer a basic goodbye isn't someone who deserves your time or energy.

HOW TO HANDLE BREADCRUMBING WITH CLARITY

If someone is breadcrumbing you, it's okay to say something. You can respond with kindness but still be direct: "I've noticed our conversations are inconsistent, and it feels like things aren't really going anywhere. I'm looking for something more intentional, so if we're not on the same page, that's totally fine."

This way, you're protecting your peace, keeping your standards high, and still being respectful. That's what etiquette is all about: clear, honest communication done with dignity and care.

USE THE COUNT OF THREE

If you don't get a response after three attempts of trying to connect with someone using the tools that a dating platform has to offer, then it's a good idea to move on.

Remember that this is nothing different than seeing someone in person. Let's say you're out and about and see someone you like. You give them a look, they give you a look, but then nothing really comes of it, and you just move on and leave the encounter alone. The same is true for online dating.

They saw you, and nothing came of it. Don't spend too much time trying to figure out what the person thinks of you and why they haven't responded after you've viewed their profile three times. Their lack of response says they're not interested. Move on and don't worry about what they may, or may not, think. Think of it this way: unless you end up dating them, or having a conversation with them later on, you'll probably never have contact with them again. Give yourself permission, then, to accept the fact that they saw you. They did nothing, so now you're going to move on.

NAVIGATING A NEW CONNECTION

Gauge timing and comfort level. Don't go out with someone if you're not absolutely comfortable with meeting them. If you have a feeling that you're just not quite ready yet, then you're just not quite ready yet. You can decline an invitation to go out on a date and continue to talk with them until you are comfortable. Never feel pressured to meet someone face to face unless you are absolutely ready.

Start with a clean slate. Avoid dragging any former relationships or experiences into this new contact. Don't start with a myriad of complaints like, "The person before you did this" or "I just want to make sure you're not this kind of guy/girl because that's who I dated before." Approach the opportunity with an absolutely clean slate.

Refrain from treating the date like a job interview. You want to learn more about the person, but you don't want to give them the third degree. Make sure that your conversation is very natural and not one of interrogation.

Use body language to your advantage. If you want them to keep their distance, then let them know with gestures that imply the need for space. Pay attention to their body language as well because that's going to tell you whether the person is interested in you. Getting in tune with their gestures will spare you from awkward moments down the line.

THE SECOND DATE

My three core values of etiquette are respect, honesty and consideration. Honesty comes into play here.

I think it's important, especially for internet dating, to be honest if you feel there won't be a second date. In my book, Let Crazy Be Crazy, I say to treat candid situations the same way you would a Band-Aid: snatch it off quickly, which means get it done and over with.

You can exchange momentary displeasure for long-term comfort. In this instance, that momentary displeasure is telling a person the following: "You know what?

It was great to be able to go out on a first date with you. I don't think this is a good fit for me. I would say that this is probably going to be our last date, but I wish you all the best in your search." The ultimate goal is to let them know that you're not planning to date them.

Remember, with dating apps, people are searching. Your purpose is to meet someone, go out on a date with them, and see if they're a good fit. Not every single date has to be a love connection. Utilize the ability to date frequently to your advantage. View the date as you would an interview based upon whether you're going to get along with the individual and if you think it's a good fit. If you don't believe it to be a good fit, then be honest with the other person and say so. That way, the person doesn't keep calling you and vice versa.

DATE NIGHT DECORUM

WHEN MEETING FACE TO FACE

- Keep in mind that this is a date, not therapy. This is not the time to unload old emotional baggage that you have accumulated in your life that may include family history and troubles. It's important for you to put your best foot forward.

- Remember to not only treat your date with respect and kindness but anyone you come into contact with as well. Also, watch how your date treats other people. This is key because we always make sure to treat our dates nicely. Let's say, however, that you go out to a restaurant and your date is rude to the server. Such behavior is a telltale sign that perhaps the person is not as considerate as they should be in terms of the way they treat others.

ARRIVE ON TIME

Be clear about your goals for the evening and the activities you have planned if you are the initiator. I would advise avoiding any other activity that doesn't allow for undivided attention on your first date. If you go to a movie, make sure you do something else so that you can have some time to talk with them face to face. This will allow you to truly see the characteristics of the person.

Five Questions and Answers on a First Time Date

1. Are there "right" or "wrong" reasons to give up on a date before it's actually over?

    •   Yes, there are some key reasons one can call it quits on a date before it's actually over. If you observe your date being aggressive and condescending towards others, it is a pretty clear indication they will eventually be the same towards you. I say RUN! Also, if your date has had way too much to drink and the night is still young, put them in an Uber and send them along their way.

2. If someone's feeling like they just can't stick it out for the whole date, what's the best way to politely let your date know that you'd like to leave?

    •   Simply say, "I think I'm going to call it a night (or afternoon or evening) and head on home now." "How about I connect with you tomorrow/sometime later?" Only ask that last question if you truly want to get together again.

3. If your date is hurt or offended that you want to leave, is there anything you can do to help them understand your feelings?

- If you choose to leave your date early, it's best to avoid trying to spend time explaining to them WHY you want to do so. It's already going to be a bit jarring that you want to end the date early, so don't add any conflict to the situation. Do not allow yourself to be convinced to stay any longer than you wish. Should they become upset, it's a good idea to leave just as soon as possible. Because you don't know the person well, it's difficult to know how they might handle adversity, and you don't want to put yourself in harm's way.

4. Logistically, is there anything people leaving a date early should make sure to do (i.e. contributing money towards the dinner or drinks bill, offering them a ride or taxi home, or something similar?)

   - If you plan on ridding yourself of the individual (and NOT ever seeing them again), then wrap things up as quickly as you can. Even if it means you put a few bucks on the bill, hail a cab, or put them in an Uber. Make your goodbye and good riddance a quick one!

5. After a not-so-great first date, what's the protocol for letting someone know you don't want to see them for another date?

   - My advice is to spare them the pain of vacillating back and forth on when to ask you out again. At some point in time, shortly after the date, contact them and be upfront by letting them know you are not interested in going out on another date with them.

CHAPTER 36

Celebrations, Gifting, and Seasonal Occasions

ENTERTAINING BY SEASON

Every season brings its own flair of celebration. Hosting during different times of the year gives you the opportunity to let your event reflect the season through color, table settings, food choices, and even fragrance. Here are a few ways you can lock in some stellar approaches to hosting throughout the year.

SPRING

COLORS & DECOR	*Soft pastels, clean whites, delicate greens. Think table runners in blush or sage, white dinnerware, and subtle accents like ceramic bunnies or floral napkin rings.*
FLORAL ELEMENTS	*Tulips, hyacinths, and peonies are perfect for this time of year. Arrange them in low vases or mix into a single statement arrangement.*

FRAGRANCE	*Light floral scents like citrus blossom, gardenia, or lavender help freshen the space and evoke renewal.*
FOOD IDEAS	*Fresh salads, spring quiche, roasted asparagus, lemon-herb chicken, and bright fruit-forward desserts like strawberry shortcake.*
BEVERAGE SUGGESTIONS	*Sparkling lemonade, cucumber water, rosé, or light wine spritzers with citrus.*
VIBE & STYLE	*Fresh, elegant, and uplifting. Everything should feel breezy and renewed. Using light layers and thoughtful simplicity will set the tone.*

SUMMER

COLORS & DECOR	*Bright citrus tones, ocean blues, coral, and crisp whites. Outdoor dinnerware, lanterns, and breezy fabrics like linen or cotton are great choices.*
FLORAL ELEMENTS	*Sunflowers, hydrangeas, and daisies. Create loose, airy arrangements or single stems in mismatched bottles for a more casual vibe.*
FRAGRANCE	*Coconut lime, sea breeze, or fresh-cut grass. Use lightly scented candles or diffusers near entryways.*
FOOD IDEAS	*Fruit skewers, grilled vegetables, chilled pasta salads, grilled meats, seafood, and easy finger foods like sliders or wraps.*
BEVERAGE SUGGESTIONS	*Iced tea, sangria, infused waters (like mint and watermelon), sparkling sodas, or citrus cocktails.*
VIBE & STYLE	*Relaxed, vibrant, and outdoor-friendly. Think effortless entertaining by the poolside, patio, or a backyard picnic.*

FALL

COLORS & DECOR	*Deep rust, burnt orange, golden yellows, and earthy neutrals. Use textured linens, wooden serving boards, and woven accents.*
FLORAL ELEMENTS	*Mums, marigolds, eucalyptus, and dried wheat bundles. Great for rustic or farmhouse-style centerpieces.*
FRAGRANCE	*Spiced apple, cinnamon, amber, or pumpkin. These can be brought in through candles, simmer pots, or stovetop potpourri.*
FOOD IDEAS	*Butternut squash soup, roasted root vegetables, hearty casseroles, apple crisp, or pumpkin bread.*
BEVERAGE SUGGESTIONS	*Hot cider, chai tea, pumpkin spice coffee, or spiced wine.*
VIBE & STYLE	*Cozy, grounded, and rustic elegance. Use layered textures and bring nature indoors through your décor.*

WINTER

COLORS & DECOR	*Metallics (gold, silver, bronze), jewel tones (emerald, deep red, sapphire), and rich greens. Velvet, faux fur, or candlelight can elevate the atmosphere.*
FLORAL ELEMENTS	*Amaryllis, evergreen sprigs, holly, and white lilies. Keep arrangements clean and bold or accent with pinecones and berries.*
FRAGRANCE	*Balsam, clove, vanilla bean, or cinnamon spice. These work well in candles or diffusers throughout your home.*
FOOD IDEAS	*Hearty stews, roasted brussels sprouts, mashed potatoes, braised meats, chocolate lava cake, or peppermint bark.*
BEVERAGE SUGGESTIONS	*Hot cocoa, warm toddies, peppermint coffee, eggnog, or mulled wine*
VIBE & STYLE	*Elegant, intimate, and full of seasonal warmth. Low lighting, soft textures, and warm drinks create a cozy, elevated experience.*

SEASONAL TABLE SETTING

You don't have to be a professional designer to create a beautiful tablescape. The thing you want to do is be intentional about your final vision and then build it out layer by layer. So, here's a simple guide to help you set your seasonal table with elegance and ease.

Start with the Base

Begin with a tablecloth, runner, or placemats. You can choose designs and colors that fit the season. This is your foundation, so choose something that has color, texture, or a pattern that fits the occasion.

Create Your Centerpiece

This can be as simple or elaborate as you like. You can use fresh flowers—some people prefer silk flowers—and greenery, candles, or seasonal items such as pumpkins or pinecones. As you build this out, keep in mind the height you're making it because you want your guests to be able to see one another across the table.

Add Your Accent Pieces

This is where you can include pops of color or style, and you can do this through your napkins, chargers, plates, and even ribbon.

Choose Your Dishes and Cutlery

Basic white is always a good standard to have. If that's all you have, it's great because you can build on it. But if you decide to go beyond basic white, you can mix and match your pieces. Don't feel as though everything has to match exactly.

Set your plates on the table with care. Place your utensils in the appropriate position. You can look at my previous chapter on dining etiquette for a diagram. Only set the table with the utensils that people are going to use. There's no need to put extra stuff.

Set the Mood

You can use lighting to create the atmosphere on your tablescape. Candles—whether they're real or battery-operated—and your overhead lighting or even string lights can help establish the tone. Figure out what you want your lighting to convey—maybe cozy, romantic, or even festive.

Add Your Finishing Touches

This is where you add in small details, such as your napkins that are folded with maybe a sprig of rosemary or handwritten place cards. Or you can print out a menu and place that at each setting. These tiny details can help elevate the experience.

GIFT SPENDING ETIQUETTE

When it comes to gift-giving, you should only spend what you can afford. Etiquette does not dictate that you spend a specific dollar amount when giving a gift. If you're ever concerned about giving something that seems too small, just remember this: a thoughtful gift, given with sincerity, is much more meaningful than something lavish or given out of obligation.

In gift-giving, you always want to give based on what you know the recipient will enjoy. That could be something inexpensive but meaningful to them.

The true spirit of giving comes from the heart, not from your wallet.

One additional point I want to add is that during the holiday season, if there's been a set monetary amount agreed upon, then stick to that. Otherwise, spending more can make others feel bad and create a rift between all parties involved.

Gracious Gifting at Gatherings

When you are attending a holiday or seasonal gathering, it's always a kind gesture to bring a small gift for the host. This doesn't have to be anything overly expensive. A small potted plant or herbs, a jar of local honey, some dish towels, or a kitchen gadget are all thoughtful choices. The purpose behind this is to show appreciation for the invitation.

Now, if you're hosting an event, it's a nice idea to send your guests home with a small parting gift. Doing so adds a special touch and leaves a lasting impression.

Here's a list of some parting gifts you might want to give to your guests:

New Year's Eve

- Mini champagne bottles with a thank-you tag
- Confetti poppers or sparklers (if appropriate)
- A journal or notepad for "New Year reflections"
- A wellness tea or calming pillow spray

Easter Dinner

- A mini loaf of sweet bread wrapped in parchment
- Hand-painted egg-shaped soaps
- A small potted tulip or daffodil
- Individual sachets of herbal tea with a springtime napkin

Mother's Day or Father's Day Brunch

- A tea towel with an inspiring quote

- A jar of homemade jam or infused honey

- A mini photo frame with a note that says, "Thanks for making memories"

- Gourmet coffee sachets or tea samplers

Fourth of July or Summer Barbecue

- Mini jars of barbecue rub or spice blends

- Handheld fans or citronella votives

- Personalized drink koozies or bottle openers

- Packets of s'mores fixings in a cellophane bag

Thanksgiving Dinner

- A small jar of spiced nuts or pumpkin butter

- A "gratitude card" with a quote and space to write reflections

- Tea light candles in a fall scent (apple, cinnamon, clove)

- A homemade biscuit or roll wrapped in cloth napkin with ribbon

Christmas or Holiday Gathering

- A wrapped ornament with the year on it

- A hot cocoa cone or seasonal cookie

- Holiday-scented sachets (pine, vanilla, peppermint)

- A hand-poured candle in a festive tin

House Blessing or Housewarming Gathering

- A small rosemary plant (symbolizes remembrance and home)
- A wooden spoon or kitchen trivet
- A candle with "bless this home" tag
- A bottle of olive oil wrapped in a tea towel

Baby Shower

- A scented hand cream with a "Thanks for celebrating with us" tag
- A wrapped cookie in the shape of a baby bottle or onesie
- A calming tea blend (especially lovely for female guests)
- A mini lavender sachet or bath soak

Bridal Shower

- A votive candle with a tag that says, "Love is in the air"
- A packet of flower seeds labeled, "Let Love Grow"
- A glass vial of bath salts or perfume oil
- Personalized nail polish bottles or lip balm

Casual Dinner or Game Night

- A handwritten recipe card with a spice packet
- A sweet treat in a small box (like a brownie or truffle)
- A themed deck of conversation starters
- A bookmark or small notepad

PRESENTING YOUR GIFTS

How you present a gift to someone matters. You don't have to be a professional gift wrapper, but you should put a little bit of effort into how it looks and how it's presented. If you have fabric on hand, you can use it to wrap something like a wine bottle. Just add ribbon and a handwritten tag. Even the simplest approach can elevate the gift you're giving. Do what you can. Take a look online and get ideas. Don't feel like you have to reinvent anything. If you see something on a Pinterest board or a blog that inspires you, duplicate it! That's why we have so many resources, so we can learn and grow from them.

GIFT-GIVING ETIQUETTE

Gift-giving has more to do with the recipient than with you. To be a great gift-giver, always select something the person will truly enjoy, rather than something you simply want them to have.

Every gift you give should be well thought out. I recommend going on what I like to call a "reconnaissance mission." Do a little bit of research to find out the person's likes and interests. You can scroll through their social media, talk to people who know them personally, or simply listen carefully to what they say. People naturally talk about their hobbies and personal interests. Let that be a guide to help you when selecting a gift for them.

GIFTING MONEY AND GIFT CARDS

Giving money as a gift is absolutely acceptable. It is a gift that is welcomed and will always be used. When you give the gift of money, be sure to put a little thought into it. Place it into a card and decorate the envelope with a ribbon, bow, or some other embellishment. Money can be given for a variety of occasions, everything from birthdays to weddings, graduations, and housewarming celebrations.

If you don't want to give money, a gift card is an acceptable alternative. Just be sure the gift card matches the person's interests. For example, if someone enjoys sweets, a gift card from a local or national ice cream or dessert place would be something they would greatly enjoy.

You can give money using a mobile payment app or service as well. Just be sure that you use the note section to let the person know what the gift is for or let the person know that it is a gift, so write something nice. One other thing you can do is follow up with a greeting card later.

DEALING WITH UNWANTED GIFTS

When it comes to unwanted gifts, there are four options: exchange it, donate it, hold on to it (for a little while), or regift it.

If you receive a gift you don't like, a vanilla-scented candle, and you know what store it came from, it's acceptable to exchange it. The same thing with clothing, perfume, or anything else. You can exchange it for a different style, scent, or color. The same applies to clothing or other items.

Donating gifts is perfectly fine as well. If an item doesn't suit you and you know it won't find a place in your life, it's better to donate it so someone else can enjoy it.

If the gift is a family heirloom or special item, such as a set of china, don't get rid of it right away. Instead, place it on hold. Keep an eye out for the perfect person who would truly treasure that heirloom.

In any of these circumstances, if the original giver ever questions what happened to their gift, the best approach is to follow the core value of respect through honesty. Be truthful. You can explain that you had someone in your life who would enjoy the gift even more. Keep your explanation simple and sincere. There is no need to go into a long-winded sob story. Now, the person might feel a little disappointed, and that is natural. Don't take ownership of their emotions. Instead, just continue to nurture the relationship with kindness. It will feel a bit awkward, but ultimately, honesty is more respectful than carrying on with a lie.

REGIFTING ETIQUETTE

Regifting, when done correctly, is perfectly acceptable. There are just a few guidelines to keep in mind. First, don't regift swag items you may have picked up throughout the year at business or social events. There's only one exception to this: if the item is extremely valuable or coveted. For example, I once attended an event where Oprah was present, and we received incredible gift bags. One item was a beautiful keychain featuring Oprah's name. I gave that keychain to my mom because I knew she would truly appreciate it, and it was in pristine condition.

When regifting, make sure the item is brand new and in excellent condition. Remove all traces of original wrapping, tags, or labels, and repackage it beautifully. You don't want the person receiving the gift to know it was given to you first.

Be careful not to regift within the same circle of friends. For example, if you receive a gift from a coworker, do not regift it to someone else at work. Keep those circles separate.

Throughout the year, as you receive gifts you may not use, I recommend setting aside a designated box at home to store them. Label each item with the giver's name and the date it was received. This simple step will help you avoid regifting mishaps later.

SECRET SANTA AND OFFICE GIFT EXCHANGES

Always adhere to the agreed-upon dollar amount for a Secret Santa or office gift exchange. Spending far more or far less than designated can make others feel uncomfortable or indifferent. The most important thing to do is to follow the company guidelines.

A good rule of thumb for professional gift exchanges is to spend about $20 to $25 unless otherwise noted. In professional settings, you should also keep gifts simple and neutral. Avoid giving anything too personal, like clothing, fragrances, or jewelry. Instead, opt for easy, universal gifts. Gift cards, outerwear items like gloves or scarves, desk accessories, or a book are all safe choices. Movie passes or restaurant gift certificates are excellent, too. The goal is to give something that feels thoughtful but doesn't cross personal boundaries.

CELEBRATING WITH GRACE

The spirit of seasonal gatherings and entertaining is about creating moments that bring people together for a greater cause. It's not about being perfect. Whether you're hosting a simple get-together or a formal holiday dinner, let your focus be on connection and bringing people together.

As you pull your event together, I encourage you to lead with kindness and be thoughtful about the experience you want people to have in your home. You want it to be stylish—but also full of warmth from your heart.

CHAPTER 37

Graduation Etiquette

GIFT-GIVING FOR PARENTS OF THE GRADUATE

Many families see graduation as a rite of passage and a worthy celebration. Some parents splurge on a car or computer. Others choose to give gifts that last, such as books, stock certificates, luggage, a camera, or jewelry, which are all presents the graduate will still appreciate in the years ahead. Choose a gift that you believe your graduate will find most useful during their immediate future. When you do this, your investment becomes more than just a gift. It will represent encouragement and support as your graduate steps into this new season of life.

TICKET DISTRIBUTION FOR THE PARENTS OF THE GRADUATE

If you are allotted a small number of tickets for graduation, here is how you can handle it. This is a common dilemma during graduation season. Explain the situation to relatives—most will be understanding. Devise some kind of plan—perhaps draw names out of a hat or invite one member from each set of grandparents to attend. You might say, "Mom, we'll only receive six invitations to Chloe's graduation. Clinton, Donna, Charita, and I are going for sure, so we'll have to decide who gets the other two tickets. It's an awkward situation. We're thinking of just drawing names out of a hat. Or do you think Dad would be willing to stay home so that you and Chris's mother could attend?" It's acceptable to invite everyone to the party even though they cannot attend the graduation.

THE GRADUATION PARTY GUEST LIST

If you're planning a high school graduation party and want to invite both relatives and your student's friends, it is absolutely possible to celebrate together. High school graduation is an exciting time for both teens and parents, so there's no reason why these groups can't mix. Get your student involved in the party planning. Let them send the invitations and plan the menu. If you're concerned about the behavior of your student and their friends, discuss this with them ahead of time. Your student should already know the polite behavior you expect, and you should already know most of their friends. Keep the conversation positive, but be sure to cover potential problems, such as noise level and inappropriate activities. And of course, be sure that no alcoholic beverages are served to minors.

GETTING GRADS TO WRITE THANK-YOU NOTES

If your graduate is reluctant to write thank-you notes, here's how you can encourage them. Appeal to their empathy. Ask how they'd feel if they put effort into choosing a gift for someone and never received a response. You can also remind them that those who feel unappreciated may stop sending gifts. A hand-written note is warmer than an email, so make it easier by providing the tools: stationery, stamps, etc. And be a good role model. Say, "How about we both sit down tonight and work on note writing?"

WHEN YOU ARE INVITED TO A GRADUATION

Graduation is a very meaningful milestone for the student and the parents. Whether it's high school, college, or some other achievement, when you're invited to celebrate with the family, it's not just about the cap and gown. This is a moment to celebrate the student's accomplishments and provide well-wishes on their new beginnings. Whether you are attending the graduation ceremony or a party or simply sending your congratulations, your thoughtfulness on this occasion will go a long way.

IS A GIFT A MUST?

If you're invited to the ceremony or are attending the party, you can either send or bring a gift, but it is not required. Gift-giving should be based upon your budget and your relationship with the graduate. If you choose not to or if your budget does not allow for a gift, then a simple card will suffice.

WHAT TYPE OF GIFT SHOULD YOU SELECT?

If you are attending the graduation in person, it is popular to present the graduate with a lei of flowers, candy, or money prior to the graduation ceremony. You can also give a bouquet of flowers afterward. If you can't be there in person for graduation celebrations, a gift delivered to the graduate's home lets them know that you are there in spirit. Here is a list of a few gift ideas:

Carry-on bag filled with full-sized toiletries and small dorm items	*Think shampoo, body wash, detergent pods, shower shoes, a sewing kit, etc.*
Laundry kit in a basket or bag	*Include detergent pods, dryer sheets, a prepaid debit card, or a roll of quarters. Include a collapsible laundry hamper and a "how-to" laundry guide.*
Personalized stationery or monogrammed notecards	*Great for thank-you notes, job applications, or general correspondence.*
Gift cards in a themed pouch or wallet	*Bundle cards for coffee shops, bookstores, fast food, or a favorite streaming service.*
"Survival kit" for college life	*A small box with pain killer, bandages, lip balm, sleep mask, snacks, tissues, hand sanitizer, etc.*
Portable phone charger or power bank	*Useful for long days on campus or travel.*
Books or journals that inspire or entertain	*Choose a motivational read or something light and fun to help them unwind.*

Dorm décor starter kit	*Think cozy throw blanket, LED lights, a letter board, or framed quotes.*
Umbrella and rain gear set	*Compact umbrella, rain poncho, waterproof tote—especially if they're going somewhere with weather!*
Alarm clock with wireless charging or Bluetooth speaker	*Something functional with a modern twist.*
A personalized keychain or ID lanyard	*Especially useful for dorm keys or student IDs.*
Sturdy reusable water bottle or tumbler	*You can add packets of electrolytes, teas, or flavored water enhancers.*
Small kitchen starter kit	*Microwave-safe bowl, mug, utensils, ramen, oatmeal packets, instant soup, etc.*
Monthly subscription box	*Snacks, self-care, books, teas, or specialty foods.*

WHEN TO GIVE A GRADUATION GIFT?

You can give the gift near or on the day of graduation. It's also fine to give it shortly after the ceremony. A meaningful gift, even if given later, is always appreciated.

HOW SHOULD THE GIFT BE DELIVERED?

You can mail the gift or drop it off in person. If you're attending the graduation or a celebration, bringing it with you is a thoughtful touch. If not, a personal note included with the mailed gift adds warmth and sincerity.

GRADUATION GIFT ETIQUETTE MYTH

"People who receive graduation announcements must send a gift."

This is a common misconception. A graduation announcement is simply a way to share an important milestone with friends and family. You are not obligated to be there, nor are you obligated to bring or send a gift. That said, if you feel a genuine connection to the graduate and want to celebrate them, you're always welcome to send a gift. Whether or not you do, a card, note, or simple message of congratulations is always a kind and appreciated gesture.

CHAPTER 38

Wedding Etiquette

Weddings bring together family, friends, loved ones, and plenty of emotions. There's so much that goes into the planning and attending of a wedding that sometimes folks can get caught up in the details and forget about the importance of graciousness and thoughtfulness. This chapter is designed to give you the basics of wedding etiquette, whether you're the one walking down the aisle or you have been invited to attend as a guest. The key thing is, it's not about rules for the sake of rules. It's really about creating a smooth, joyful experience for everyone involved.

WEDDING ETIQUETTE FOR THE COUPLE

ANNOUNCING YOUR ENGAGEMENT

Before posting the news about your engagement on social media, take a moment to personally tell the inner circle of your life. This would include your parents, grandparents, and any close family members.

A quick phone call, FaceTime, or text message will go a long way in making sure that everyone feels included in your excitement.

COMMUNICATING AN ADULT-ONLY WEDDING

The best way to communicate that children are not invited is through the invitation itself. When addressing invitations, you can omit children's names. Whether it's a paper invitation or electronic, you would convey that information there.

A simple way to phrase it is:

"This is an adult-only affair."

or:

"Adult Reception."

Try to avoid phrases like "No children allowed," as it may come across as too harsh. Some couples get more creative and say something like:

"We'd love to celebrate with all the adults in the room. We encourage you to make other arrangements for your little ones."

You can also have friends and family spread the word discreetly.

Where to Include This Information on the Invitation:

- On the RSVP card – guests see it as they confirm their attendance.
- At the bottom of the invitation – below attire details.
- On an enclosed insert – a separate note in the envelope.
- On the wedding website – include the same wording for consistency.

MAKING AN EXCEPTION FOR CERTAIN CHILDREN:

If you plan on including select children, communicate it privately:

"I just want to let you know that we will not have children at the wedding, except for your daughter [niece's name]."

For children in the wedding party, set up a kids' table or hire a sitter.

PROVIDING CHILDCARE FOR GUESTS:

Include the details about childcare on your wedding website or on a separate insert with the invitation. Designate a point person at the event to welcome families and help facilitate the childcare services.

HANDLING GUESTS WHO ARE UPSET:

If someone complains:

"I'm sorry that our decision has hurt your feelings, but this is a one-day occasion for us as a couple, and this is how we would like to celebrate."

Stick to your decision gracefully.

HANDLING PLUS-ONES

It is acceptable for you to limit plus-ones. The general guideline is that you should offer a plus-one to someone who is married, engaged, living with their partner, or in a long-term relationship. You're not obligated to give every guest a plus-one, but the key is to be consistent and make sure that your guest list and the invitation wording reflects your intention.

GIFT REGISTRY

You're not required to create a gift registry, but you have to think about this: the registry is not necessarily for yourself, it's really to help your guests. Often, when people are purchasing a wedding gift, they don't know what to do or what to purchase.

Some individuals are really great gift-givers and can pinpoint exactly what to give. Others need some guidance, and so that's where your help comes in.

If you prefer not to have a gift registry for whatever reason, I recommend that you take into consideration the individuals who are invited to your wedding. If you have folks who are from an older generation who enjoy the tradition of purchasing a wedding gift, then you can register for some items that you need. You can select small things that can be useful around the house.

You don't have to have a registry with towels and sheets and plates and utensils. You can have a registry that has something to do with starting a home garden or perhaps some home improvement items. Choose some things that are useful and that you'll actually enjoy.

MONETARY GIFTS

Brides and grooms look very different nowadays. Some folks may be on a second or third wedding, or perhaps they've been living together already and have already established a household. Or maybe they're just getting married a little older and they don't need all of the stuff.

And with that, it is acceptable to ask for money. Just make sure it has some sort of purpose behind it. Whatever that purpose is, designate it and tell your guests exactly what it is. You can share this on your wedding website or the insert to your wedding invitation.

Etiquette dictates that it is acceptable to ask for money as a wedding gift. The focus is to make sure that the monetary request has purpose to it. For example, you might be asking for guests to contribute to a honeymoon fund or perhaps contributing to home improvement.

I have a couple rules in terms of asking for money, and here they are:

- Use word of mouth via family and wedding party.
- Never print cash requests on the invitation itself; use a separate card or website.
- Accept physical gifts graciously, even if money was preferred.

SENDING THANK-YOU CARDS

A handwritten thank-you note for wedding gifts is still the gold etiquette standard. Send thank-you cards within two to three months of the wedding. If you leave for your honeymoon immediately after your wedding, it's all right for you to write your thank-you notes upon your return.

A good practice is: if you begin receiving gifts prior to the wedding, start writing the notes and send them as you receive them. This way, they don't pile up. I talked about the proper elements of a thank-you note in the earlier communication chapter, and the approach is the same. If you receive money, you follow the same guide.

HOW TO WRITE A THANK-YOU NOTE FOR A MONETARY GIFT

- Write the person's name.

- Say the words "thank you."

- Name the amount of money you received.

- Say something about the gift they gave you.

- You can make a statement about your gratefulness.

- Or, you can say what you will do with the money.

- Sign your and your spouse's name at the bottom of your note.

> *Dear Benita,*
>
> *Thank you for the $200 monetary gift.*
> *Your thoughtfulness and generosity helped*
> *contribute to us having an enjoyable*
> *honeymoon.*
>
>
> *Love,*
> *Beverly*

SETTING TECH AND SOCIAL MEDIA BOUNDARIES

If you want a tech-free wedding ceremony and/or reception, it is most certainly your prerogative to do so. The popular term for a tech-free wedding is an "unplugged wedding." This phrase generally refers to the ceremony only, but in some cases, it applies to the entire event.

The purpose is to encourage guests to refrain from using their phones, cameras, or other electronic devices. The goal is to help everyone be fully present, minimize distractions, and avoid interfering with the professional photographers.

You can let your guests know about your unplugged wedding in advance. This can be done through the wedding invitation, on your wedding website, or with a sign placed at the entrance.

Here's how you might word it:

"We kindly request no photos during the ceremony. We want to see your faces, not your phones."

"Welcome to our unplugged wedding. We invite you to be fully present with us during our ceremony, so please turn off all phones and cameras."

ASKING FAMILY FOR FINANCIAL SUPPORT

If you're hoping your parents or loved ones will contribute to the wedding, approach the conversation with respect and clarity. Schedule a time to speak privately. Express your hopes and ask what they're comfortable contributing.

Don't assume that they're going to pay for the entire wedding or a specific portion. Be prepared to adjust your plans based on the answer they give.

Here are a few ways to phrase your request based on your level of need:

Asking for a general wedding contribution:

"We're in the early stages of planning and would love to talk with you about our wedding budget. We're hoping that you might be able to contribute to the wedding in a way that would be comfortable to you."

Asking parents to pay for a specific vendor:

"We've identified a few key vendors that are really meaningful to us, and we were wondering if you might be open to helping us by paying for one of them."

Asking to split the wedding cost equally:

"As we start budgeting, we're trying to find ways to cover the costs of the wedding. Would you be open to discussing the idea of splitting costs evenly between both families? We're hoping to keep the process collaborative and low-stress for everyone involved."

Asking if they can contribute at all:

"We're setting our budget and wanted to check in with you early on to see if you would be willing to contribute in any way. We completely understand if now isn't the right time, but we wanted to give you the opportunity to be part of the planning, in whatever way feels right to you."

MANAGING FAMILY PARTICIPATION EXPECTATIONS

Although it's a kind gesture, there is no etiquette rule that says you're required to ask your fiancé's family to be one of your wedding party attendants. If someone expresses interest in being involved, it's all right to decline, but be proactive just in case you receive a negative reaction.

You can offer an alternative role so they still feel included. Perhaps they can do a special reading, act as an usher, or handle the guest book. You can also ask them to wear the same colors as the wedding party so they feel connected to the celebration.

OPTING OUT OF A BRIDAL SHOWER

If you don't want a bridal shower, be sure to convey your wishes early to the person who offers. Simply thank them and be gracious, but stand firm in your boundaries. You can say:

"I'm so grateful for your excitement, but I've decided to skip a traditional shower this time."

"I really appreciate your love and support, but I prefer to celebrate in other ways."

CAN YOU INVITE AN EX?

The short answer is: yes.

The long answer is: if you are cordial with one another and your fiancé is comfortable with it, then yes, you can certainly invite your ex. This often comes up when small children are involved and the ex is part of the child's life or may even participate in the wedding.

The most important thing is that both the bride and the groom agree fully that the ex can attend.

WEDDING WEEKEND ETIQUETTE

If your celebration is a full-on weekend or destination event, make sure that you provide all the details clearly. Let your guests know what's happening each day. This information can be shared on a wedding website, and you can also use your wedding party to help spread the word.

HANDLING PARENTS' ROLES

Parents should avoid over sharing wedding details on social media. A helpful self-check is this:

"Is this a memory for me or my child?"

If parents tend to over share or tell embarrassing stories, couples should have a pre-wedding conversation to avoid any mishaps during the reception.

Parents should also communicate openly with the couple about guest lists and wedding roles early on to prevent misunderstandings later. A good way to ask might be:

"I know that you have your own guest list, but I'd like to know how many people your dad and I are able to invite."

HOW TO ADDRESS ENVELOPES FOR WEDDING INVITATIONS

When addressing wedding invitations, it's important to reflect courtesy, clarity, and respect. Here's a comprehensive guide covering all the most common and a few unique scenarios:

SINGLE GUESTS

Single female

- *Ms. Jane Doe*

Single male

- *Mr. John Doe*

COUPLES

Married couple, same last name

- *Mr. and Mrs. Mark S. Wood*

Married couple, different last names

- *Mr. John Doe and Mrs. Jane Smith*

Dating couple, different last names (not living together)

- *Ms. Jane Doe*
- *Mr. John Smith*

Unmarried couple living together

- *Ms. Jane Smith*

- *Mr. John Doe*

- *(listed on separate lines, no "and")*

Same-sex couple

- *Mr. John Doe and Mr. James Doe*

- *or Ms. Jane Doe and Ms. Jill Smith*

GUESTS WITH PROFESSIONAL TITLES

Female doctor and spouse

- *Dr. Jane Doe and Mr. John Doe*

Male doctor and spouse

- *Dr. John Doe and Mrs. Jane Doe*

Both are doctors (same last name)

- *Drs. Jane and John Doe*

Both are doctors (different last names)

- *Dr. Elaine Swann and Dr. Christopher Swann*

Female judge and spouse

- *The Honorable Jane Doe and Mr. John Doe*

Male judge and spouse

- *The Honorable John Doe and Mrs. Jane Doe*

Both are judges

- *The Honorable Jane Doe and The Honorable John Doe*

RELIGIOUS TITLES

Pastor and spouse (same last name)

- *Pastor and Mrs. John Doe*
- *or The Reverend and Mrs. John Doe*

Pastor and spouse (different last names)

- *The Reverend John Doe and Mrs. Jane Smith*

Female pastor with spouse

- *The Reverend Jane Doe and Mr. John Doe*

Two religious leaders (married)

- *The Reverend John Doe and The Reverend Jane Doe*

Catholic priest (single)

- *Father John Doe*

Rabbi (single)

- *Rabbi John Doe*

Rabbi and spouse

- *Rabbi John Doe and Mrs. Jane Doe*

Imam and spouse

- *Imam John Doe and Mrs. Jane Doe*

MILITARY TITLES

Active duty (male)

- *Sergeant Clinton Gorham Jr., U.S. Marine Corps*

Active duty with spouse

- *Captain John Doe, U.S. Army and Mrs. Jane Doe*

Retired military

- *Master Chief William A. Wood, U.S. Navy (Ret.)*

Female service member and spouse

- *Major Jane Doe, U.S. Air Force and Mr. John Doe*

Both are military officers

- *Major Jane Doe, U.S. Air Force and Captain John Doe, U.S. Air Force*

FAMILIES AND CHILDREN

Family invited with children by name

- *Mr. and Mrs. John Doe*
- *Jack and Jill Doe*

Entire family invited

- *The Doe Family*

INVITING A GUEST WITH A PLUS-ONE

Female guest with a plus-one

- *Ms. Christie Gorham and Guest*

Male guest with a plus-one

- *Mr. John Doe and Guest*

WEDDING ETIQUETTE FOR THE GUESTS

RSVP ETIQUETTE

Respond promptly. Don't wait until the last minute. The bride and groom are relying on this information to help plan their wedding. This includes the meal count, the favors for guests, the seating, and table decor. Even if you're not attending, respond to let them know. If you miss the RSVP deadline, expect that your spot may be given away.

DECLINING A WEDDING INVITATION

It's okay to say no to a wedding invitation, especially if it's someone you don't know quite well. This happens often in the workplace, where people may invite colleagues out of courtesy.

If you decline, utilize the method that the couple provided, whether it's an RSVP card, email, or online portal.

You are not required to purchase a gift unless you feel moved to do so. If not, a simple wedding card will suffice.

CAN YOU REQUEST A PLUS-ONE?

If your invitation does not include a guest, that means the couple has made a decision not to offer one.

There are some instances when you might want to bring a plus-one. For example, if a family member is visiting from out of town during the wedding or if you simply don't want to attend alone. Your plus-one doesn't necessarily have to be a date; they could be a friend or sibling.

My recommendation is: ask the couple politely if you're permitted to bring someone and always be prepared for their answer. If the answer is no, accept it graciously.

And if you're bringing a plus-one simply for the sake of having a date, don't just bring someone random from a dating app. Keep in mind, this is a wedding, and the photos are forever. You want someone you actually know well standing next to you in all your "forever" pictures.

Remember, the couple has made intentional decisions based on their guest count, their budget, and personal reasons. We must respect that.

NAVIGATING A WEDDING SOLO

Take time to think before declining. It might ultimately be a good decision to attend.

If you do decide to attend:

- Be supportive of the couple.

- Help where you can (carry the bouquet, assist elderly guests).

- Try to connect with other singles who you know are going in advance.

- Be prepared with a humorous story or fond memory to share.

- Give yourself permission to leave whenever you feel like it.

- Drink moderately—you don't want your behavior to become the story of the wedding.

CAN YOU BRING YOUR CHILDREN?

Only bring your children if they were explicitly invited. If your invitation does not mention them by name, or if it's addressed only to you, then assume it's an adult-only event.

If you're unsure, just ask. But don't show up with your kids unannounced. And try not to be offended if the answer is no.

FOLLOWING THE DRESS CODE

This is one of the easiest ways to respect the couple and their vision for the big day.

If a dress code has been given, follow it. If not, make your best judgment based on:

- The **time** of day

- The **location** of the ceremony and reception

- The **personality** of the couple

- The **style** of the invitation

These details will give you an idea of what's expected. For example, a grand evening venue with printed invitations likely calls for formal attire. A garden wedding? Something light and airy.

If you can't get a clear perspective from the couple, ask a member of the wedding party or the family.

DO YOU HAVE TO BUY A GIFT FROM THE REGISTRY?

It's not required, but it's thoughtful and it's the best way to avoid giving a gift that ends up in the back of someone's closet or donated later.

The wedding gift registry is your guide to buy something the couple will use. If you choose to purchase something else, make sure it's meaningful and appropriate.

Always purchase a gift based on what you believe the couple will enjoy. If you're a great gift-giver, go for it. If not, follow the registry.

WHAT IS A DESTINATION WEDDING?

A destination wedding is a celebration held in a location away from the couple's hometown or the city where they live. It typically requires most guests to travel and arrange overnight accommodations.

But destination weddings aren't limited to tropical beaches or international destinations. They can happen anywhere that's meaningful to the couple and far enough away that travel becomes part of the experience like a vineyard, a mountain resort, or a charming coastal town. Key elements of a destination wedding include:

- The venue is not in the couple's hometown.

- Most guests are required to travel and stay overnight.

- The celebration takes place over multiple days and includes several events (like a welcome dinner, excursions, or a farewell brunch).

GIFTS AND DESTINATION WEDDINGS

At a destination wedding, you're already spending a significant amount to travel and take care of accommodations. In this case, your presence is often considered the gift.

That being said, it's acceptable to send a card to the couple's home or offer a small token of celebration, but you are not expected to purchase a traditional gift.

TAKING PHOTOS AT THE CEREMONY

It's good practice to avoid taking photos during the ceremony. Stay out of the way of the photographers and be present. Enjoy the moment through your eyes, not your phone.

The couple will appreciate your undivided attention.

Of course, it's acceptable to take photos of yourself before or after the ceremony, and many couples set up designated photo areas for that. But during the ceremony itself, just be fully present.

SOCIAL MEDIA ETIQUETTE FOR WEDDING GUESTS

If you take photos at the wedding, especially during the reception, don't post photos or videos of the couple before they do. Let them have the joy of sharing their special day with the world first.

Once they've posted, feel free to join in the celebration. It's fine to post photos of yourself—just wait until the couple has shared theirs first.

If the couple has asked you to use a wedding hashtag, use it! There's a reason for it. They're curating memories from the guest experience, and using the hashtag is just another way of giving them a gift.

CEREMONY AND RECEPTION SEATING

At the ceremony, traditionally guests of the groom sit on the right and guests of the bride sit on the left. But weddings have evolved, and you may find a sign that says, "Sit wherever you like."

If so, pay attention to reserved seating signs and fill in the space. Don't sit all the way in the back. Fill the seats so the couple can feel the love.

At the reception, don't assume you can sit wherever you like. The couple may have designated seating areas, and once you've received your assigned seat, don't change it.

Reserved seats are typically marked for immediate family and close loved ones.

AVOID BRINGING UP THE COUPLE'S PAST RELATIONSHIPS

If you're asked to speak at the wedding, keep in mind that a wedding is a celebration of love between the couple and their future, not a time to bring up the past.

Even if you have a story that shows triumph or "how far they've come," this isn't the time. Keep it light, positive, and forward-looking.

ASK BEFORE TAKING CENTERPIECES

As gorgeous as the centerpieces may be, don't take them without asking. Some are rented or reserved for specific guests.

Don't assume they're free to take. If you'd like to take home a floral arrangement, check with a member of the wedding party or the family. Don't bother the couple on their wedding day. This isn't the time to ask questions about what can or can't be taken. They're likely focused on soaking in the moment, greeting loved ones, and enjoying their celebration. If you're unsure about something, use good judgment and be discreet.

Be thoughtful and respectful. Let the day remain centered on the couple and their joy.

Etiquette is about showing up with grace and leaving with it, too.

WITH GRACE AND STYLE

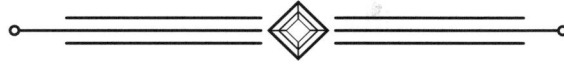

Thank you from the bottom of my heart. As we wrap up this part of our journey through modern etiquette, it is my hope that you walk away not with just a set of rules but with a renewed sense of purpose—a purpose rooted in respect, compassion, and care for those around you. Etiquette is not about being perfect. It's not about being fancy. It's really about being thoughtful towards others. It has to do with how we move through this world with intention. How we make others feel seen, valued, and respected. It's how we show up for our family members, loved ones, friends, colleagues, strangers, and even ourselves with kindness and grace.

Whether you're navigating the workplace, your everyday life just out and about, hosting a dinner, planning or attending a wedding, sending an email, or simply saying hello in passing, know that your presence matters and how you show up in this world matters. Whenever you are in doubt, I encourage you to lead with kindness. Thank you kindly for allowing me to be part of your journey, and I hope this book serves as a trusted companion and resource that you'll return to again and again. I encourage you today and always to approach everything you do with grace and style.

Warmly,

Elaine Swann

MEET ELAINE SWANN

Elaine Swann is a Panamanian American entrepreneur, etiquette expert, and cultural thought leader. Third in a family of five siblings, she developed a love for etiquette early in life when her mother gave her the daily responsibility of setting the dinner table. That simple task sparked a lifelong fascination with refinement and grace. Her mother later enrolled her in charm school, and Elaine continued her education in etiquette through Girl Scouts, pageantry, and formal training, beginning with her senior year of high school.

Following graduation, Elaine moved to New York City to pursue a modeling career. While there, she launched her first business, E.P. Models, a model management company that represented petite models, many of whom landed principal roles in popular music videos. After returning to California, she attended cosmetology school and opened her own hair salon in 1993, serving clients while nurturing her creative instincts.

While running the salon, Elaine also worked as a freelance creative art director for Today's Black Woman Magazine and contributed as a writer for Word Up Magazine, lending her artistic voice to publications focused on Black culture, fashion, and entertainment.

In 1996, Elaine made a pivotal career move and became a flight attendant with Continental Airlines, where she gained invaluable experience in global hospitality, discretion, and grace under pressure.

During this time, she continued to operate her hair salon while also completing Continental's International Protocol and Etiquette Training, which laid a formal foundation for the work that would come next.

In 1997, a sorority, aware of her pageant and etiquette background, invited Elaine to train participants for their annual debutante ball. What began as volunteer work quickly became a calling, and for the next five years, she returned each season to develop and deliver increasingly advanced etiquette instruction. In 2002, a local middle school principal booked Elaine to develop an after-school etiquette program for students. The response was immediate and affirming.

In June 2003, Elaine officially closed her salon and launched her etiquette business under the name The Etiquette Advantage Institute, turning her passion into a business that would shape the next two decades of her life. For ten years, she also offered day-of wedding coordination services, blending etiquette with celebration planning for couples and families.

Elaine married Christopher Swann, an accomplished professional musician, in January 2005. The following month, in February 2005, she auditioned for The Martha Stewart Apprentice in San Diego. Though she didn't make the final cast, her on-camera interview with NBC caught producers' attention. In May 2005, she was invited back for an on-air etiquette segment with NBC San Diego. Her first stint was such a hit, it led to a three-year relationship with the station as their resident etiquette expert. During this time, Elaine often went straight from the morning news studio to the airport to work her flight, frequently selecting San Diego layovers to manage both careers with dedication and style.

In 2007, Elaine made the bold decision to leave Continental Airlines and dedicate herself full-time to her etiquette consulting business. Her media presence continued to grow, with national appearances on The TODAY Show, CNN, and a range of other television and digital media outlets. Her expertise has also been highlighted in The Wall Street Journal, The New York Times, Oprah Magazine, Essence Magazine, and Real Simple. She is the author of four books and has led corporate training sessions for global companies including Merrill, Cisco, and Bank of America, and has spoken at premier institutions such as Stanford University and The Wharton School. Her relatable, real-world advice earned her the title "The Emily Post of the Digital Age" from The New York Times.

In addition to her business and media work, Elaine appeared as a contestant on the FOX reality competition series Kicking and Screaming in 2017, where she and her teammate advanced to episode seven out of eight. The experience highlighted her adaptability and grace under pressure in a physically demanding environment, further showcasing the poise and perseverance that define her work.

That same year, she rebranded her business as The Swann School of Protocol and launched a comprehensive certification and licensing program, allowing others to open their own Swann School locations under her guidance. Today, The Swann School of Protocol has multiple independently owned and operated locations across the United States, bringing etiquette education to communities nationwide.

Elaine has also served on the boards of several nonprofit organizations and continues to use her voice to support causes that reflect her values of education, empowerment, and community service. In 2014, she was licensed as an Evangelist Missionary and actively serves in ministry leadership, mentoring women and supporting regional faith initiatives.

At the heart of it all, Elaine is a devoted wife, mother, and grandmother. She is married to Christopher Swann, and together they are the proud parents of their daughter Sequoia Gorham and son-in-law Clinton Gorham, and find endless joy in their grandchildren: Chloe, Christie, Clinton Jr., and Colton.

Elaine is known among her loved ones for her warmth, hospitality, and love of entertaining at home. She treasures time spent with her family, close friends, and inner circle, especially during her favorite holiday, Thanksgiving, when the table is full and fellowship runs deep. A lifelong avid reader, Elaine draws joy and inspiration from the written word, much of which has shaped her own journey as an author and educator.

With over 20 years of experience, a nationally recognized etiquette brand, and a powerful media platform, Elaine Swann has redefined what it means to live with grace, confidence, and common sense. Her legacy is not just in what she teaches but in how she lives it.

THE SWANN SCHOOL
OF PROTOCOL

The Swann School of Protocol is a nationally recognized etiquette training institute founded by Elaine Swann in 2003. Built on the belief that etiquette is not about perfection, but about consideration and confidence, the school provides modern, relevant guidance for navigating today's world with poise.

What began as a single program under the name The Etiquette Advantage Institute evolved into a full-service academy serving children, teens, college students, professionals, and executives. In 2017, the school was rebranded as The Swann School of Protocol, and a comprehensive certification and licensing program was introduced. This expansion empowered individuals across the country to establish their own Swann School locations, bringing high-quality etiquette education to communities nationwide.

Today, The Swann School of Protocol has multiple independently owned and operated locations across the United States, offering a wide range of classes, workshops, and private trainings. From professional presence and communication to dining etiquette, social grace, and digital decorum, the school equips individuals with the tools to lead with confidence and kindness in any setting.

At the heart of the Swann School philosophy is the idea that etiquette is more than table manners. It is a pathway to empowerment, a bridge between cultures, and a skill set that enhances both personal and professional lives. With a modern approach rooted in timeless values, The Swann School of Protocol continues to set the standard for etiquette education in the 21st century.

GRATITUDE AND LOVE

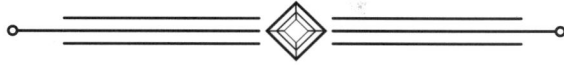

First and foremost, I thank God, my Heavenly Father, for the wisdom He has given me and for the opportunity to share this gift with the world. I am grateful for every door He has opened, every mountain He has taken me over, and every valley He has brought me through. I am deeply grateful to my Lord and Savior, Jesus Christ, who is truly the head of my life, who has ordered my steps and given me the gift of salvation.

To my husband, Christopher Swann. Thank you for walking beside me with unwavering love and encouragement.

To my daughter, Sequoia Gorham, and my son-in-law, Clinton Gorham. Your support and belief in me have meant the world.

To my grandchildren, Chloe, Christie, Clinton Jr., and Colton. You are my greatest joy and the light of my legacy.

To my mother, Betty Lee (in loving memory), and my father, William A. Wood Jr., thank you for laying the foundation of who I am.

To my loving stepfather, Walter Lee (in loving memory), and my father's dear wife, Bebiana Wood. Thank you for your presence and support throughout my life.

To my siblings, William A. Wood III, Beverly M. Clark, Mark S. Wood, and Vernetta S. Shine. Your presence has shaped and strengthened me.

To my in-laws, Jerry and Nina Swann, and my sister-in-law, Benita Swann. Thank you for embracing me with love and kindness.

To Dr. John Sanders. Thank you for your leadership, strategic insight, and early investment in the company. Your wisdom and vision helped shape its foundation and mean the world to me.

To my dear friends and extended family. Thank you for your encouragement, prayers, and presence along the way.

With gratitude and love,
Elaine

INDEX

Z

Kayppin Media
Parkland, Florida

Library of Congress Control Number: 2025939265
ISBN: 9781962447287 (Hardcover)
First Edition, 2025

Printed and bound in China

This book is a work of nonfiction and is based on the author's personal experience and professional expertise in the field of etiquette. Any names or identifying details may have been changed to protect the privacy of individuals.

Interior Layout: Waheduzzaman Manik
Interior Design and Art Direction: Clinton Gorham | The Gorham Agency
Cover Design: Clinton Gorham | The Gorham Agency
Copy Editing: Heather McAdams
Illustrations: Jeiel Media
Photography: Tim Otto Photography

For permissions, licensing inquiries, or to contact the author for speaking engagements,
Please visit www.elaineswann.com